Advance Praise for *Lo*

"Mental illness is a topic that many people don't want to talk about. It takes a great deal of courage to not only speak and share the information, but also to be an advocate for someone that can't be one for themselves.

"In her book *Lost and Found* Linda Denke takes on the role of parent, advocate, storyteller and educator who helped her son from being lost to being found with her support in his recovery. It is a must read for anyone, whether they have someone they know and love suffering from a mental illness or not."

—Judy Hoberman, President, Selling In A Skirt

"A compelling read, a true story, as a mother simultaneously searches for her missing mentally ill son, stigma, bias, and prejudice against her son, against her, surface, as does confronting how three generations of mental illness affected her life."

—Harold G. Koenig, M.D. Professor of Psychiatry &
Behavioral Sciences

"Incredibly honest and compelling, Linda Denke has beautifully depicted the despair and devastation that comes when mental illness strikes. Her story of motherhood and her journey with her son is one that candidly describes sorrow and hope as she experiences the real life, daily battles that inevitably come when your child has a mental illness. Anyone who has known and loved someone with a mental illness will connect with her lived-experience; gathering strength from her experiences and hope that not only survival, but recovery is indeed possible."

—Rebecca Deisler, BSN, RN, PMHN-BC,
Clinical Manager-Psychiatry,
University of Texas Southwestern Medical Center-Zale
Lipshy University Hospital

"I got totally immersed in reading Dr. Denke's account of her journey through her son's mental illness in *Lost and Found*. Her ability to share her fears, struggles, hopes and dreams with such candor provides an opportunity for the reader to gain an empathy and understanding that surpasses what can be learned from a textbook on the subject of bipolar disorder. On the other hand, the scientist in Dr. Denke also reveals information which assists in transforming and elevating the reader's understanding of these very complex illnesses leading to an awareness that recovery is not only possible, but likely when appropriate treatment is sought. My personal hope is that more people will display the kind of courage that Dr. Denke and her son John have shown in sharing their personal stories to help others. We now know that hearing the stories of people with lived experience can offer hope and healing for others who are currently struggling with these illnesses. Thank you, Linda and John!"

—Sherry Cusumano, RN, LCDC, MS,
Administrative Director of Community Education and
Clinical Development, Medical City Green Oaks Hospital

"This is a poignant memoir of a mother struggling to accept that her family members, including her son, have or had mental illness, and overcoming her internalized stigma and bias. She persevered for the sake of her son who could count on her help and support to reach recovery, which he has done. Along the way she and others in her family learned some profound truths about themselves and about mental illness."

—Yvonne Broach, a mother whose son
is diagnosed with a mental illness

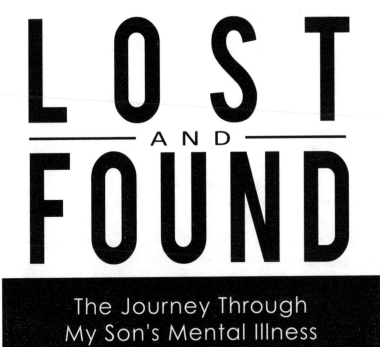

LOST
AND
FOUND

The Journey Through My Son's Mental Illness

LINDA M. DENKE

A SAVIO REPUBLIC BOOK
An Imprint of Post Hill Press
ISBN: 978-1-64293-061-0
ISBN (eBook): 978-1-64293-062-7

posthillpress.com
New York • Nashville
Published in the United States of America

DEDICATION

This book is dedicated to my son John, to his strength, courage, and immeasurable love, and to mothers like me whose sons are diagnosed with a mental illness.

FAITH

"Now faith is the substance of things hoped for, the evidence of things not seen." Hebrews 11:1

TABLE OF CONTENTS

PREFACE

WE FOUND YOUR SON

"Mrs. Denke, this is Officer Paul Johnson. I'm a police officer with the Aventura Police Department. I'm calling about your son John. We found him on I-95 outside of Aventura, near Miami, Florida. A truck driver called us and reported a young man, who we later learned is your son, was wandering down the middle of the interstate. The driver of the truck reported he almost jack-knifed to avoid hitting him. I'm sorry to be the bearer of bad news, but he's now being transported to Aventura Hospital, as he appears to be dazed and unstable. Is he being treated for a mental problem?"

When I heard the words, "police officer" and "John," the floodgates opened, and memories of the past five years rushed into my awareness: phone calls, cold and impersonal courtrooms, crowded staircases, elevators, security, police, sheriffs, black-robed judges, and the pain that accompanies everyday people like me during sudden, unfortunate circumstances. Past visions played like a film in my head. Up and down the stairs and hallways, from one hospital to the next, passing self-absorbed doctors and indifferent nurses. This flood of recollections refused to fade. My downward spiral began the day John walked out the door and disappeared. I held those memories secret, deep inside my dark soul, until they eventually roared into the light. John's mental illness was an unbridled horse. It was indiscriminate and worrisome, and remained difficult to harness. Words tried to escape when I attempted to express my pain, but they would freeze on the tip of my tongue. Petrified and unable to move, I disengaged from life. After many years of waiting for my pain to stop, the disease of depression erupted and gripped me. I braced myself for the worst. My nightmares replayed and were full of vivid, horrific scenes starring my son, the truck driver on I-95, and Officer Johnson. This tragic news plagued me for years.

OOO

This is the story of my son John, who was diagnosed with bipolar disorder in 2005 when he was twenty-three years old. It traces his journey to recovery from his random trips overseas, to jail, to seemingly endless hospitalizations, when he went missing, homelessness, and financial disaster.

This is also the story of my experience as a single mother as I walked hand in hand with John through the course of his illness. It traces my own journey to recovery from hopelessness, extreme anger, severe depression, and fear while attempting to live in the world. I sadly had to face and confront my own denial; my own destructive, embarrassing bias against mental illness; and find the almost nonexistent support to bring my son—and myself—back to sanity.

This is not a how-to handbook. It's not an everything-resource book. It was written for you, the reader, so you might find hope in the midst of facing mental illness, whether in yourself or a loved one. You might even discover a new meaning and purpose for your life, like I did. I want you to know what it is like to be confronted with a mental illness condition, especially if you're a single mom facing this crisis alone.

My journey began years ago when I was oblivious to mental illness. *Lost and Found* contains the lessons I learned as I fumbled around in my mind and blindly navigated the world alone trying to save my son and myself from losing our minds. I was lost as to what to do and where to go when my son became ill. It is my sincere wish that you will come away from this memoir with a better understanding of mental illness and what you can do to save yourself and your adult child with mental illness. I would like to make it a little easier and less earth-shattering through reading and learning from my mistakes and triumphs.

I want you to know that it *is* possible to find what you thought was lost forever.

CHAPTER 1

WHO AM I?

March 2007

Barreling down I-95 at eighty miles per hour is Jared Livingston, a five-foot-nine, sturdily built veteran of the Iraq War. His brown hair looks like the standard military crew cut soldiers are required to have. He is clean-shaven and well-groomed, as one might expect for an ex-military guy. His left arm is tanned from hanging out the window on sunny days while on a delivery for a customer. He still follows the rules and regulations of the Marine Corp. He is a nice enough guy, and no longer smokes thanks to a Department of Veterans Affairs' physician who prescribed a nicotine patch. Jared rarely smiles. His demeanor is stoic and serious. Mission first with a no-nonsense attitude.

He is a full-fledged, full-time driver for ABF Trucking and has been for six months now. Near the end of his last delivery of his day, his high beams shine right into John's eyes, making them glow red in the dark night. Charging ahead at eighty miles an hour, there seems no way to avoid hitting my son. Jared slams on the brakes anyway. Jared grips the steering wheel furiously and attempts to swerve left, then veers off the road. This is the near-death collision that changed our lives forever.

○○○

Fifty-one days had passed since my beloved son John disappeared before the highway incident. He had walked out the front door and vanished. Where? This was anyone's guess. The night after I received the phone call, the nightmares started. Between my restless sleep, nightmares, and cold sweats, was violent shaking. Did I ever sleep? Would I ever rest again?

Before John went missing, I rarely woke up at night unless I was stressed at work from dealing with patients and their families. I would worry about all the unfinished nursing care that often goes undone, like washing hair and listening to my patients' concerns, yet I learned to leave those worries at work. After John went missing, my sleep brought me dark horrors and the nightmares replayed. The images of flashing headlights in the dark on the interstate, the sounds of cars and trucks speeding along, a truck driver desperately blowing his horn, and my son's wide, frightened eyes swirling around in my sleep.

My part in all this was simple. I kept vigil. I had a PhD in keeping vigil. I didn't set the alarm anymore since I quit trying to sleep after 4:00 a.m. I would get up and walk around to pass the time. It was March 8, 2007, when I got that call. It was still dark outside and nothing mattered anymore. That was my life, my routine then. My life was safe and structured before my son went missing. It will no longer be the truth.

My life turned upside down when my son went missing. I understood what this cliché meant, and I knew it was better to accept what was happening in the moment. But I focused on the raw numbness from fear of the future. My inner routine started as soon as I awoke. My worries followed the same pattern. I would wonder where my son could be. Was he safe? Did he have clothes on and food to eat? Was there anyone looking after him? Was he stranded somewhere? Was he hurt from being mugged, beaten, assaulted, or, God forbid, left for dead on a highway? Had someone murdered him?

The worry transmuted into sheer panic that wouldn't go away.

Sometimes I crawled into bed during the day to nap from pure exhaustion. I still worried. I found that I couldn't read my body signals anymore, whether I was tired or hungry, nor did I really care. I was losing myself and my ability to cope.

After the call from Florida, my dreams became more detailed night after night. There were swirling images on the interstate. Next the loud voices of the truckers would begin, some with heavy accents. They discussed which cops to avoid, the latest accidents, highways with construction or detours, which truck stops were easiest to maneuver, and the restaurants with the best food. Their conversations signaled the beginning of an earth-shattering scene, which played again and again, with the same ending.

The sounds would become louder. And then, the crescendo: the eighteen-wheeler zipped along, brakes screamed, the tight swerve, the hard skid across the lane, all in slow motion. Black skid marks would burst into small flames then a smoke cloud would descent over the terror on John's face. I heard the insidious thump, and his lifeless body was tossed in the air like a rag doll. The next scene was the 911 call for help. The siren screams got louder, the EMTs scattered. That was when I would wake up, gasping for air.

My son was almost killed by an Iraq War veteran named Jared. He saw John walking aimlessly from out of nowhere, in the middle of I-95 South heading toward Miami.

My heart was dead, devoid of joy. My life was meaningless. That nightmare became my new reality. My son was lost to me twice. Once when he walked out the door when he went missing for months, and again, to severe mental illness.

CHAPTER 2

GENETICS

My ex-husband, David, and I grew up in a small town in Pennsylvania. My mother not only knew everyone, she made it perfectly clear to me that David's mother, Rose, was mentally "off base." Since David and I were an item, I spent some time at their house. Their home was difficult to get to. It was located off a steep highway, down a hill, and was the second-to-the-last house along an unpaved road. It was nearly impossible to navigate the driveway and walk up to the front door when it snowed. Plows never came to clear the road as far back as I can remember.

The house was an early sixties-style dwelling and totally uninviting. It was surrounded by unkempt trees, overgrown bushes, and tall grass that blocked the sunlight. Darkness hung over the house like a widow's shroud. There was a heavy emptiness there, and I thought the house was haunted.

There were telltale signs that something was amiss with Rose. She was my first introduction to someone with mental illness. Naturally, like any new experience, I was curious, and had no idea she was diagnosed with a disorder until long after I began dating David. She never drove a car, and never left her hometown except for her honeymoon. Her sad energy never failed to greet me at the door. I would enter the same scene every time I visited. Nothing ever changed, not even during the holidays. She was always in her own world sitting in a ragged blue chair in front of the television. She rarely looked up to talk to me. While my mother had plenty of knickknacks, Rose lacked a personal touch. Nothing but ashtrays could be seen on the kitchen counters and on the few tables scattered about in the living room. At least that was all I viewed upon entering that house through the side door. I was young, but I did notice what was missing were framed photos highlighting her children's milestones and group family photos. I do remember one lone photo on a dusty table in a dark hallway, a black-and-white photo of Rose singing on stage in a nightclub. Before she married, she was a singer, and quite popular. She was beautiful with her long, shiny ebony hair, dark skin, and even darker eyes. She was wearing a slightly revealing vintage V-neck gown. The Rose in that stunning photo in that lonely hallway was a stark contrast from the Rose I saw then. It was like she was two different people in one life.

Rose smoked continuously, and the house reeked of cigarettes. Smoking for her was her job, her routine. She often lit at least six cigarettes while I was there, though she finished none. I detested the cigarette smoke, and it made me cough, but I was polite. I waited for her to light the cigarette and watched her stare off into the room until the cigarette required her to flick her ashes before they fell onto the carpet or dinner plate.

Once she was standing in front of the television, rambling something nonsensical about the FBI, when she burst into laughter for no real reason. Although she was not much fun to be with for more than a couple of hours, she was harmless. The more time I spent with her, the more accepting and relaxed I became. After all, David and I had been close since high school, and we dated every weekend. Sometimes she accompanied us to Ted's Diner for lunch or dinner. I would tread lightly and keep an eye on her. But mostly I would fixate on David to look for signs that her behavior was beginning to change. The pressure of watching and waiting for sudden changes in Rose was exhausting. It seemed as if it were David's job to smooth her out when she was acting strange in public. She wreaked havoc in David's life while he was in high school, and in her ex-husband's life, but I never witnessed it.

Back then, her condition was labeled manic-depression. It was often treated with psychotherapy and lithium. I don't remember if Rose went to therapy or not because David never talked openly about her condition while we were dating. There weren't many outpatient clinics or state hospitals at that time either, at least in that part of Pennsylvania. Just the thought of knowing someone with a mental illness was socially disturbing. Embarrassment replaced concern because of the stigma. Sometimes she seemed relatively normal, and eventually I learned those were the times when she took her medication with consistency. But she couldn't tolerate the side effects of lithium, so she would stop taking it, and things would get tough in her family. David hinted about trouble but never in detail. His mother's mental state made her unable to form and maintain healthy relationships with her children, and unfortunately stunted their emotional development. I know this personally because I married one of her sons. I just had to figure it all out.

I always sensed a deep chasm between Rose and the rest of her family. Being a son with a mentally ill mother must be a terrifying experience. David suffered in silence, and put his pain, embarrassment, and shame in a box. I learned to build a wall between myself, Rose, and my suspicions of mental illness in my ex, and eventually my own son when their symptoms or strange behaviors appeared.

I constantly questioned myself about what I was seeing and intuiting. Surely Rose was just a quirky and eccentric woman. I know she suffered alone. As far as I know, she talked to no one about her feelings except the occasional trip to her doctor. Long after David and I started dating, it finally dawned on me that she was, without a doubt, mentally ill. While I didn't want to face the reality that one of my offspring would inherit the genetic predisposition, it occurred to my mother. She was a fine nurse and a curious student in school. She was up-to-date on the new research studies regarding the relationship between mental illness and genetics, and she would share this information with me in a hinting sort of way. I didn't listen. I was dead set on marrying Rose's son.

CHAPTER 3

A SON

My mother kept slipping me information about genetic connection to mental illnesses, even after David and I married. She also hinted that David seemed "somewhat off" as well. She said there was "something in his eyes." I blew off her comments at first. But her words started to haunt me, so I started reading and researching about mental illness. I must admit, although my fear that my firstborn would carry the predisposition for bipolar disorder slowly unfolded from the background into my consciousness, the joy of a new life overrode my concerns. In addition to my mother's hints, I was around Rose a lot more than I was when David and I were dating. While it was clear to me that Rose was strange, I could sometimes walk around or hop over the wall I had built between us to protect myself from the shock of some of her behaviors. At times, Rose was hysterically funny, especially during one of her manic episodes. We would laugh so hard together. I learned to love her. She would bring the family together with her exuberant energy and her eagerness to please. There were times she invited us to her famous dinner parties where she would cook authentic Lebanese cuisine. We'd walk into her kitchen filled with steaming pots while she flurried around to please us. Rose introduced me to stuffed grape leaves and kibbeh. She was the impetus for me falling in love with her culture. Inevitably, she would retreat and hide in silence and sadness for weeks sometimes. I naively thought her condition was hers and hers only, so how could it rub off on me? How could it affect her son who seemed to be a totally different person with extremely different values? Yet I was always on edge, especially when we were in public together. I was embarrassed by some of her behaviors. My own stigma and biases about people with mental illness began to unconsciously emerge into my once open, non-judgmental mind.

Despite the odds of having a child with mental illness, I became pregnant by our first anniversary. We didn't plan that pregnancy because we were married, young, and naïve. I wanted to be a good wife and please my husband. I thought that if we maintained an ideal marriage, we would always be going in the right direction.

My son John was born on July 6, 1981, in Dallas, Texas. He was a beautiful child with the face of an angel. He instantly became the love of my life, and I was convinced that any mother would have been proud to claim him as her own. He had this way of gazing into my eyes, like he possessed an innate sense to see deeply in my soul. His intense stare seemed to pierce right through, like a laser. I was convinced that he possessed great intelligence, an old soul who would grace my life with unimaginable truths. And he did.

John never crawled, but rolled across the carpet and onto the hardwood floors. He was a head banger, which I found disconcerting. When I confronted his pediatrician about these behaviors, he said that it was a phase and he would soon move on from it. There was nothing to worry about from what he could tell after his regular examinations. And it did stop. Yet in the back of my mind, John's head-banging episodes raised red flags in me for years.

John was often in his own world, his gaze fixed, staring at the swaying pecan trees outside our living room window. He was content to spend hour after hour during the day, with me nearby, staring out the window. He loved watching the squirrels scurry around in the leaves or leap from tree to tree. I would watch his eyes follow the activities of the wildlife. He would be tightly wrapped in his handmade blue blanket studying the outdoors while I went about with my chores.

John was innately shy and pensive. He was a model student, no matter what school he attended, and spent most of his time growing up buried in books. He started kindergarten earlier than most of his peers because his birthday was in July. We thought about holding John back to allow him to enter kindergarten the following year, but he wanted to start school. He was engaged from the first day of class and consistently performed extremely well in all his classes each year.

John loved to spend time with my father. His Grandpa Joe was a workingman and invited John and his brother, James, to work at his car wash/laundromat at young ages. Every morning during the summer, John, James, and Grandpa Joe would head out the door, kiss their grandmother goodbye, and begin their summer work routine.

The laundromat was a quick drive up Main Street, where my parents lived. The houses along the way were built in the 1930s, some even earlier than that. They dotted the street inbetween Bennie Davis Men's Clothing Store where my mother bought all my father's suits for special occasions. The drive is the same now, and hasn't changed much since I was a little girl, save for a daycare center named Little Ones.

My father's truck was never clean, and for someone who owned a car wash, this made little sense to me. Newspapers and money sacks, along with plain-old, brown coal dust, littered the floor. Coal dust was everywhere in northeastern Pennsyvania. On Sundays, unless it was raining, which it did most of the time, he spent time before church vacuuming the truckseats and floor mats so Mom didn't get her clothes soiled. He was a kind and thoughtful man.

The 1960, dark orange Chevy truck as my dad's favorite "office." Mom kept that truck even after Dad got leukemia. When he was seriously ill and unable to drive, people who saw his truck around told stories about him and how he was a "man's man."

The townees called him "Carwash Joe," as he is still remembered today. Whenever my siblings and I visit the area, my mother introduces us to some new neighbor. They always smile and say, "I knew your dad, Carwash Joe. He was such a good man." I beam every time I hear this from anyone. My brother and sister feel the same.

I learned the routine when I worked at the carwash as a young girl. Taking care of Prince, my father's German Shepherd, was my job. Prince served one role: he was a guard dog. Because Prince was friendly and docile, my dad often joked about Prince's obliviousness to danger around the premises. Prince was a loving dog. When my father, and my brother and sister and I spent the day at the car wash, we all jumped in the truck and drove from my parents home. The moment we pulled up to the car wash, I opened the truck door and I jumped from the truck to where Prince was chained to the stake near the entrance. Prince eagerly would tug at his chain to greet me. I would always give him a pat on the head and embrace him. He would jump all around me like my prescence was long overdue.

The boys carried their lunches every day. They loved ham sandwiches and peanut butter and jelly sandwiches, so these were on the menu each day and mother made them. The laundromat smelled of detergent and fabric softener. Each morning, John and his brother picked up the clothes that were strewn over folding tables, the floor, and in wastebaskets. The boys would gather stray socks or a lone shirt or two and fold them nicely so the clothes could be picked up later by the owners who'd left the items behind.

They emptied the coin boxes, swept the floors, and tidied the laundromat. They counted the candy bars and pop cans left in the vending machines. Their list of chores varied depending on how messy the floors and machines were from the day before, or whether it was a weekend, when more people wanted clean cars and needed clean clothes.

One several occasions, John filled the machines with candy and sodas depending on how many were missing from the day before. He would unlock the closet where the inventory was kept. Grandpa Joe let the boys grab a candy bar and can of soda for later, unless he was in the mood to surprise them with ice cream before heading back home.

After they finished the list, the next task of the day was to wrap the coins they had collected that were left in the machines. The boys took the coins, piled them into cloth coin bags with the name of the bank stitched in gold letters on the outside of the bag, and headed to the house to count them. Finally they would go to the bank, bags and all, to make their deposits. Although the boys were not paid directly for work, Grandpa Joe allowed them to pick up all the dropped coins that fell under the table and pocket the change. It was funny, because Grandpa Joe would "accidentally" drop most of the coins. By the end of the summer, to their delight, the boys came home with well over fifty dollars each to deposit into their bank accounts.

Every summer, beginning at age eight, John traveled the United States with his brother and father on adventures to places such as Yosemite National Park, the Grand Canyon, and the O.K. Corral. I looked forward to checking the mailbox to find postcards from their adventures. Each postcard ended with "We miss you, Mom!!"

John and his brother spent many summers with Grandpa Joe and Grandma Marie. They learned to like large metropolitan cities like New York, Philadelphia, and Atlantic City. These cities held a fascination for John, and he found his way to these cities before he would return home. His brother studied at Fordham University in Manhattan, where Grandpa Joe taught at one time.

John loved New York City and his face would light up when he described the city sights and sounds. He would be so excited when he spoke of the traffic, wall-to-wall people, beeping horns, the cabbies, and other noises of the city while in route to the Empire State Building. John always mentioned that Grandpa Joe would grab three hot dogs with everything on them before they went on a cruise around the Statue of Liberty. The summers brought rest for me and adventures for my sons. When they returned, I was always happy to see them, but I was truly grateful for the break and time for myself.

My heart smiles every time I think about the wonderful childhood my children were fortunate to experience. I was sure my children were loved and cared for by many people other than me. John and his brother's travel experiences always delight me because not only are they fortunate enough to travel throughout the United States, but internationally, to England and Spain. Between my parents and their father, the boys traveled to forty-eight states before high school.

My sons are the loves of my life but they are as different in temperament and in personality as night and day. John had a normal childhood. He behaved and navigated his world with ease and sanity. How did he get this illness? How did it come about? Did I unintentionally repeat a destructive pattern that hurt him in his heart? What did I do?

CHAPTER 4

TELLTALE SIGNS

AFTER JOHN'S DIAGNOSIS, many people, including John's doctors, asked me if he exhibited signs of bipolar disorder during childhood and adolescence. There was a lot of concern on my part due to this disorder on his father's side of the family, but nothing in John's behavior stood out as being abnormal. He was well behaved, quiet, and kept to himself most of the time. Looking back, I realize that he didn't veer much from a typical boy who was reserved and curious about the world around him. His gentle, calm nature had a soothing effect on me. He was a model child. However, during John's childhood, something big was going on with my husband David.

My sons were born thirteen months apart. I was a busy, busy mother. David began to show signs of mental deterioration in our early years of marriage. I began to feel more isolated and alone as I desperately tried to hide his mental state, and the way it affected me, from everyone. I had two people whom I loved in my life with all the signs of mental illnesses for whom I had to care: my husband and my mother-in-law. Let me explain. Although my ex was never diagnosed with a mental illness, his behavior became more and more erratic during our marriage and I believe the trigger of his mental deterioration began with the birth of my son John. His condition worsened with the birth of James, although this is my perception of the circumstances surrounding my marriage and my ex. The oil business was in jeopardy and so was his business, because of the high interest rates for borrowing money and mortgage loans; we had financial problems during this time as well. This was also the worst time for my ex to start his own business, and leave all of the security of his position as a geologist for an oil and gas exploration company behind after being employed with them for seven years.

David was becoming more and more unpredictable and was no longer the husband that I could lean on or live with. His spending was out of control, and the state of his business was unknown. His behavior was erratic, and disturbing. I started living in a state of quiet fear behind a wall of isolation. I was constantly smoothing out David's strange behaviors that he acted out in front of the children. Sometimes he became so angry he threw furniture and raged verbal assaults in front of the children. Strangely, David didn't even acknowledge his condition, making me question my own sanity. It never occurred to me to seek help or call the police. It became a huge family secret. That was how it was back then. All things less than ideal were kept behind closed doors.

This ideal childhood I thought my sons lived may not be the case at all. In fact, their travels and time with my parents began after I divorced, and it was my parents' way of showing their love for me and my sons. My sons' travels with their father started simultaneously as they went to visit my parents in Pennsylvania and often the boys traveled the entire summer. James and John were three and four years old, respectively, when I divorced their father. I was in survival mode and my state of mind was focused on two things: saving as much as we could that we worked so hard to get and keeping my sons safe. My home was in foreclosure, the housing market had plummeted, and I was desperate. When the first offer on the house arrived, I took it. I gave up my hopes and dreams of creating a normal family when I handed over the keys to the house we'd once called home.

I was under constant pressure with my new responsibilities. I was a single mom and the main breadwinner. I worked every chance I got to make ends meet. I experienced a lot of guilt and shame because I spent little quality time with my sons. When I was with them, it was to get them ready for bed or to get them prepared for the day with a caregiver. Often I had three jobs to pay the bills and to provide my sons with the lifestyle they deserved. Sometimes I became despondent and angry due to that hectic and demanding lifestyle. I wanted these feelings to disappear, but they didn't. I got to the point where my anger and frustration were affecting my work. I was terrified that I might inappropriately lash out at the staff at work or at my children. I knew that I needed help to ease this pressure. Did this contribute to John's illness?

My ex had visitation privileges but often disappeared for months at a time from our lives. I later learned he traveled to China and various other places, supposedly looking to explore for oil. Therefore, he distanced himself from his sons and I was more relieved he did, because I worried he was not able to care for them to my standards nor did I know whether or not my sons would be safe in his prevue. So several years passed before his reappearance in their lives once again and this time, he was in a relationship with a younger woman. This relationship proved to be a good thing for us because the relationship seemed to stabilize him for a while, or he was very different when I lived and was married to him. Once the boys were in middle school, my ex reappearance, was a relief and unsettling at the same time for my sons and me. Later I realized the fact that I was terrified my ex may have a mental illness. This fact was one of the main reasons I contemplated divorce from a man I loved but wanted to be as far away from as I could get was to save my sons from this fate. Today, I realize my fear of mental illness was paralyzing, and I did everything I could to put this fact, of my son's predisposition to mental illness was real, out of my mind. I would not have to face my beloved sons may one day elicit the same fear I remember I experienced with my ex, with them as their mental illness showed up one day at their front door.

I was referred to a counselor after I attended a divorce seminar offered by two counselors who happened to be married to each other. Bryan, my counselor, was a godsend. He shed light on my options to go forward with my new life. He really saved me from myself, but not so much from my shame. As a practicing Catholic, divorce is taboo. Nobody discussed divorce in the church in the 80s. Bryan always reassured me that there were successful single-parent homes, and as a woman it was possible I could raise my sons right in that environment. I decided to turn my anger and helplessness into a positive endeavor to go forward to parent my children with joy. As it stands today, I'm the only one who is divorced in my immediate family. This fact still stings, no matter what I do to push it down.

The "typical" signs of the manic phase of bipolar disorder—agitation, sleeplessness, rapid speech—didn't appear in John. The odd behaviors seemed to manifest themselves in my other son, James. He was strong-willed and gregarious. He was also a hellion, disruptive, rowdy, and vigorous. John was a rule follower. James seemed to outdo and outshine every child he associated with, especially his brother. He was unpredictable and assertive, while John stood by and watched.

When I look back in my current frame of mind, I think John showed the "typical" signs of the depressive phase of bipolar disorder. When he was in elementary school, he was shy and quieter than most of the children in his class. His distant behavior didn't impact his learning or home life, so

I didn't worry all that much. We all went to counseling after the divorce, and the counselor didn't point out any abnormal behavior. I wish she had spotted something, as this might have spared John the crisis he was to face in college.

When John reached puberty, he began to stay awake all night for periods of time. I wasn't too concerned about this because his main goal since kindergarten was to succeed in school. He always studied and consistently earned straight As. He was never disruptive in school, and no strange behavior was ever reported from a teacher. In fact, he was never angry or violent. He rarely raised his voice. Even during the throes of intense symptoms, he remained kind and compassionate.

I tentatively began to watch for signs of mental illness when my sons reached their teens, especially following their father's behavioral change. I don't recall ever being alarmed by any abnormal behaviors. The strange thing about John's bipolar disorder is that it manifested powerfully in college. When his illness began, it resulted in a full psychotic break, and my watchful waiting mode instantly morphed into nurse and care-giver. That was when everything went into warp drive mode.

CHAPTER 5

COLLEGE

JOHN WAS A stellar student when he turned nineteen. His grades assured us a predictable glimpse into his future success. He was the kind of kid who listened to adults, and he usually heeded their advice. This character trait led him to high aspirations and excellent grades. He had compelling scores on the SAT and LSAT.

John decided to move in with his father while he attended the University of North Texas. UNT was forty miles from his father's house, but John was willing to commute. He wanted to be closer to his father since he didn't see him much when he was in middle school. They were very close in temperament and had some of the same daily habits. John reassured me often that he was happy and content with his living situation. I didn't see him much during this time.

My son decided not to work during his breaks since they usually lasted one month. We encouraged him to rest and rejuvenate so he could concentrate on his main job, college. We instilled in John and his brother that school performance was a habit, and goals can be reached with study and focus over time.

My parents supported my siblings and me in college, even though we were encouraged to work during our summer breaks. One summer I worked in a Bazooka bubble gum factory, about forty minutes up the road from my parents' place, and often tell this story to make us all laugh. I would say that I was Laverne in the television show *Laverne & Shirley.*

Working in a factory was hard. I wore a hairnet and heavy, heat resistant gloves. I made penny Bazooka gum with the comic strip in each one of the wrappers. My job was to splice strips of gum together, then feed them into the hot wheel so the ends of each string melted and stuck together to form an uninterrupted string of gum. My mother often cajoled me to tell the story of when I worked for Bazooka. She and her friend would laugh hysterically. Even today she laughs and drowns me out before I can finish telling the story.

My life was consumed by a job as a nurse when my boys left the house for college. I was under the impression that John was going to make the transition to law school with ease. The future looked bright for my sons. They were likely to secure scholarships and would need much less financial support from me. I had no doubt they both would be able to support themselves and their future families. I was hopeful, and secure for all of us, as opposed to the grinding financial anxiety from being a single working mother most of my sons' lives.

Planning for my own future seemed like a lost possibility since I was so focused on making ends meet. Taking care of myself was a foreign concept to me. I didn't have a social life, nor did I even think of dating. After my sons went to college, I had inspirational flashes of continuing my education. Nursing was fulfilling, but options to branch into other areas were limited without a master's degree. Teaching was something I had always wanted to do. Eventfully I discovered the path that would lead me into my own future life. I imagined myself with a PhD in the role of a teaching professor, conducting research, and perhaps writing a book someday. I began to see myself in a state of financial security, doing a job that I loved. The void I vaguely felt in my heart was gradually filling with excitement.

I had hope that I would discover some consistency in a possible future life for me.

The comfort of predictability slowly fades when you have a child with an undiagnosed mental disorder. Because John studied in Advanced Placement classes in high school, his second year at UNT was his final year. John was well on his way to law school with only the entrance exam to go before he applied to law schools.

It stood to reason that he wanted to be like the other students. My son started hanging out with a couple of kids who introduced him to the college scene. He began drinking and doing drugs with his roommates. His alcohol abuse and periodic drug use with those friends eventually triggered his bipolar disorder. One of those roommates disappeared, and John later learned that he was homeless and lived in his car. His friend had spent his entire hundred-thousand-dollar college inheritance on drugs and alcohol. Another roommate dropped out of college and periodically reached out to John for free legal advice for his misdemeanors. John helped his former friends with friendly advice, but never took him on as a paying client. That's how kind he's always been. Recently, John attended the funeral of this wayward friend. He learned he was murdered over a confrontation with a woman. Maybe John, even with his bipolar disorder, had the better life.

I didn't know it then but one of the most difficult challenges with a son like John is building and sustaining friendships. During his early school years John had few friends his own age. His newly found college friends brought some excitement, but it didn't last. Although he still insists he's an introvert and likes being alone, it's difficult to think about since his father and I will eventually pass on. He just might not have his own family.

I asked John throughout his life if having little or no social contact bothered him or made him sad. He always told me that he preferred his own company. I feel the same way. I'm fiercely independent. John and I have always been very close, and we see each other regularly during each week now. John is happy just the way he is. His major company is his father, brother, and me. His passion and favorite pastimes have always been writing and cooking.

Despite the partying, John managed to keep his grades up. His father enjoyed his parenting role, and both were quite content, so I did not intervene. Since he was on target to graduate, no news was good news. After all, John had graduated thirty-second in his high school class of over twelve hundred students.

One day during semester break, I stopped in to say hello to John and take him to lunch.

Out of the blue John declared, "I just made thirty thousand dollars in the stock market!"

"What are you talking about you made thirty thousand dollars in the stock market?"

"Yeah. I was day trading the past couple of weeks. Dad loaned me three thousand dollars up front. I was up to one hundred twenty thousand dollars, but I lost that. I stopped at thirty grand. My profit," John answered.

"So what are you going to do with the money?" My mind raced. My heart buzzed. I became so confused and uncomfortable as I tried to comprehend this.

His story sounded unreal. How does a twenty-two-year-old with no formal knowledge in business or stock market trading parlay several thousand dollars into thirty thousand dollars?

"Yeah, I know it's weird," he laughed. "I'll pay Dad back and buy a car so I can get to and from school in a new ride. I am looking at an Acura."

I had no reason not to believe my son even though I strongly felt that this was totally out of character. I thought that perhaps he was just pulling a joke on me, so I brushed it off. I never saw a new Acura. However, several years later, while gathering and sorting his documents, after his illness and hospitalizations, I saw a statement from the IRS. I stared at the document with disbelief. The income reported to the IRS was thirty thousand dollars, right there in black and white.

I was always proud of both my sons and their achievements. Yet I sensed a frightening change in the air. Was my son displaying gifted traits or some quirky new way of thinking? Eventually my vigilance to discover the truth paid off. I realized that these eccentric behaviors were none other than the beginnings of some sort of mental illness.

The whole idea of the words "mental illness" frightened me. If I hadn't married into a family with a history of mental illness I might have saved John from it. Regardless of the futility of changing the unchangeable, I continued to obsess over that. I longed to believe that if I replayed this scene, if I kept my sons far away from my ex and his mother, I could somehow prevent them from slipping into a mental illness, enough times, the outcome of John and now James succumbing to a mental illness, would be different.

Slipping into my mind to reshape my reality didn't work as well as it did in the past. The decision I made to have a child many years ago couldn't be undone. Nevertheless, John has always been my shining star.

Within the next couple of years, the events that took place were overwhelming. The son I knew and loved gradually disappeared, and there was nothing I could do to stop it from happening. Nothing.

CHAPTER 6

LAW SCHOOL

JOHN WRESTLED BETWEEN becoming a physician or an attorney. He finally decided on law school and applied. He was accepted into two law schools, New York Law and Loyola New Orleans College of Law. I persuaded him to attend the latter, a Jesuit college located not far from me or his dad.

One of the reasons John agreed to accept this offer was because he was extended a partial scholarship. His father had encouraged him to attend the school which gave him the scholarship. While he attended the University of North Texas during his undergraduate work, he kept his expenditures to a minimum, receiving his degree in two years after high school. When John decided to attend law school in New Orleans, he took out one hundred twenty thousand in loans total if you add the loans he already took out for his undergraduate degree. My dream for my son was one step closer to being realized.

If I have learned anything about bipolar disorder, it is that drugs, alcohol abuse, and my son were a lethal combination, especially since he eventually admitted he was self-medicating. Therefore, using occasionally in college and continued use of alcohol and other substances in law school proved to be the "beginning of the end" for my son.

I often wonder if the pressure of law school, school loans, and the college scene early on triggered his psychotic break and his eventual diagnosis of bipolar disorder. I understand that drugs and alcohol are a wicked combination in a child who has a predisposition for mental illness, but the added stress could have been the final factor. It's difficult to pinpoint the true reasons or the combination of reasons why my son's mental illness manifested. I wish I truly knew. Maybe I could have lessened his burden somehow. I was focused on my wish for John to be successful in school and life.

Fifteen years after school, John was working non-stop and took on the responsibility to pay off his school loan. He continued to make regular monthly payments to honor his loans. Although his financial situation was healthy, I always wanted to help my sons more than I was financially able to in the past, so in August 2017, I paid off the remaining balance of John's law school loans. John was happier than I had seen him in many years. He called his brother James, who was ecstatic as well. But of the three, I was the most thrilled. I felt the financial burden lift from him. My entire family could now feel the effects of what it means to be debt-free.

As a parent, I had less and less influence in my son's life. It was common for me to hear from someone else that John was in a crisis. The events that occurred beginning a couple of years into law school were the beginning of devastation in our lives. No one could have convinced me that my beloved son, the child that I loved with all my heart, would be in the New Orleans parish jail. John slowly became someone I did not know or even recognize. As the events unfolded my panic and fear increased. My life became chaotic. A mental illness diagnosis brings a life of unpredictability. The worst part about this state of slow deterioration is that while a child over eighteen years of age still needs intervention, when your child reaches the age of eighteen he is considered an adult and must give his or her consent to all medical treatments. For John to recover from his bipolar disorder and me to be involved, I desperately needed to know his medical condition. John always consented to treatments and as a courtesy, he gave his consent for me to have all access to his treatments and medical records. Having access provided me with many of the details in this book, and some clues as the illness unfolded.

CHAPTER 7

NEW ORLEANS

November 2003

I WAS IN my car on my way south to New Orleans. It was fifty-two degrees and the weather was perfect for a football game. In fact, fifty-two degrees in November was much warmer than any day I knew while growing up in Drums, Pennsylvania. I was no stranger to the ice and snow that accompanied the winter months in December, January, and February. Fall in the Northeast is unpredictable, but not so in New Orleans.

The weather, the drive, and my excitement were a combination that created an elation in me I hadn't felt in a long time. I was going to attend a New Orleans Saints game. The Saints were playing the Denver Broncos later that day at the Louisiana Superdome, which had been renamed the Mercedes Benz Stadium after Hurricane Katrina in 2011. This was my first Saints game, and I was thrilled to have the time off from work. This was also the first time in a long time that I had saved enough and put aside money for an event.

New Orleans held a certain fascination for me, and I decided I wanted to learn as much as I could about New Orleans, the Saints, and the Louisiana Superdome. As a history buff, when I planned a trip or conference, especially to somewhere I had never traveled, I researched the destination city or town. This football game was no exception. First, I've only been to a few professional football games. Second, I am a workaholic. I rarely take time off when I can afford to do something I consider frivolous. I would rather have the security of savings in the bank. So this was a big step for me to take time and money away from my usual routine and step out of my comfort zone.

I conducted an inordinate amount of research about the city and its unique history during the months before my trip. I was going to learn all I could before I set out on my road trip. There is a mystery that surrounds New Orleans. I'm certain I am not the only one who feels this way.

There are many interesting features about this city. I became fascinated by the aboveground cemeteries. I am naturally drawn to any cemetery wherever I travel. The writing on the headstones reveals many interesting facts and assumptions about the individual resting there. A quick glance at a headstone reveals the individual's birthdate and the year of death. Another interesting fact is the size of the headstone and where it is located. This indicates what position the individual played in the family and if the graves of family members are buried together. If I see a large, ornate headstone that towers above the others, I can surmise that the family was well off and revered the individual. The headstones range in years across decades, and in some parts of the country, such as New Orleans or cities in the Northeast, a century. There are many facts I gathered from cemeteries over the years during my travels. New Orleans was no exception.

My parents regularly read the obituaries as they had many friends and acquaintances, and attended many funeral viewings. They would discuss the deceased, how they knew them, and planned their day around the viewing. My parents normalized death. Eventually I did so as well. I was always comfortable with death, which explains why I was drawn to oncology nursing. It is no wonder that I have an attraction to cemeteries. I didn't attend my first viewing until my grandmother on my mother's side passed away. I was twenty-two years old when my favorite high school biology teacher died. I felt more prepared and less anxious. I was confident about going to the viewing, and I vividly remember that experience. I think this curiosity about death led me into the nursing field. How can I help prevent it, and how can I respect death once it inevitably happens?

During my research, I discovered that New Orleans cemeteries are known as "Cities of the Dead." The Girod Street Cemetery was originally located under parking garage number two of the Superdome. The cemetery was established in 1822 for Protestant residents and consists of 1,100 tombs. Saints fans never blamed a losing streak on the players, owners, fans, or the coaches. They believed the Saints were haunted by the souls in the Girod Cemetery upon which the Superdome was built.

I had six tickets for the game: one for my son, three for his roommates, and two for my friend and me. I was thrilled to attend the game with my son. That year was his first year in law school. He was only twenty-two years old. The sun was bright but there was a chill to the air. My son and I sat side by side and cheered the Saints under a black-and-gold sports blanket. The fans were screaming and chanting along with John and a couple of his suitemates he'd invited to come along. John was so happy and centered. This is one of the happiest memories I ever had with John during law school. Little did I know at the time that our happiness would be so short-lived.

CHAPTER 8

ARRAIGNMENT

November 2004

No one could have told me, based on John's college performance, that he would end up incarcerated. On the day I learned he was in jail, I went to work at my job as a nurse and a clinical research coordinator. I was the nurse site coordinator for the Principal Investigator for Colonoscopy Feasibility Study, which was originated by researchers at Memorial Sloan Kettering Cancer Center. Since this was a feasibility study, it was my responsibility to recruit and enroll patient volunteers to participate in the research study.

This was an ominous task, or so the research team thought. Who would want to volunteer to have a colonoscopy? To everyone's surprise, one of the environmental services housekeepers volunteered, and afterwards, her coworkers and other housekeepers soon followed suit. Our research physicians realized that a diverse sample is generalizable and would favor the outcome of the study results.

We posted flyers, and the individuals who enrolled recruited their husbands and wives, brothers and sisters, church members and neighbors. All agreed to volunteer and participate. My best source of recruitment surprised the team because volunteers are known for recruiting other patients by word of mouth. The other research sites were enrolling patients at a slow but steady rate, but we enrolled close to our goal numbers not long after we started recruiting participants.

During lunch, I decided to turn on my cellphone. There was a voice message from Eric, my son's roommate. The message said that John had been arrested the previous night for drunk and disorderly conduct. He was scheduled to be arraigned at 9:00 a.m. The public defender wanted me to call him.

I placed a call to Eric. He was, and still is, a good friend to my son. He's a good kid with a kind heart, just like John. He met my son during their first year in law school. They became friends from the time they met. Eric explained that they both were at a party drinking the previous evening, where John had met a girl. He apparently thought they were getting close as they spent a couple of hours in an intense conversation. The girl left before them without saying goodbye. John decided that he would go to her apartment to ask if she would like to continue partying. Apparently, the girl wouldn't answer her door, and John kept on knocking and making a ruckus. She called the police, and he was arrested for drunk and disorderly conduct.

I was furious at my son, and surprisingly, at myself. My fury was displaced onto my ex-husband, my son's roommate, the public defender, the police, and God. My mind raced with these thoughts, but honestly, I was ashamed, not only for my son, but for me and my family. Somehow all this was my fault. If only I had spent more time with John and stayed with my ex-husband, it might have made John more confident in himself. I still struggle with conflicting emotions about the divorce and my children's well-being.

John always idolized his father despite his shortcomings. I was grateful that I made up my mind early on, after my divorce, that I would refrain from saying anything harsh or despicable about my ex-husband. After all, I cared for him at one time, and had learned, over time, to respect him as a person. We were just totally opposite in nature and disposition.

"This is George Arceneaux. I'm a parish public defender in New Orleans, Louisiana. Your son John was arrested last evening for drunk and disorderly conduct. I understand that John is a student at Loyola Law School? These things happen when law students need to blow off steam from time to time. Really, it's nothing to worry about. He will be arraigned at nine in the morning. You can take him home after you post bail."

The public defender's voice was surprisingly relaxed.

The words "post bail" reverberated in my ears. My throat tightened, and I couldn't speak for what seemed like an eternity. My heart pounded. I began to perspire. I knew my body was signaling a fight or flight response, and honestly, I wanted to run. I was near hysteria.

My son, who was always a model student, was arrested for drunk and disorderly conduct. To my dismay, he was housed in the Orleans Parish Prison while awaiting his arraignment. I didn't really know the definition of an arraignment. Once my initial shock wore off, and my fear subsided, I became enraged. What was he thinking, and how in the world could he be arrested for drunk and disorderly conduct? Was the simple act of knocking on a door to ask a girl out disorderly? How could he be out at night on a Tuesday with class next day?

Because John had no priors, the public defender said this would not likely be a problem for him. I remember thinking that was the end of it, that there would be no more issues. In time, John did assure me that this was, in fact, true.

The next thing I knew I was in Orleans Parish Prison, sitting in the Orleans Parish public defender's office. I was embarrassed and humiliated, mostly for myself. I was sure that that public display was worse for my son. The public defender spoke rapidly. He had a classic New Orleans accent, which was pleasant sounding with a distinctive cadence all its own. He realized I was uneasy and required some direction about how I was to behave, and more importantly, how to proceed with this unexpected event. The public defender assured me that if we paid the fine, all would be well.

Regardless, I had a feeling of impending doom, even though Mr. Arceneaux assured me that everything would soon be back to normal. I wanted so much to believe him. As it turned out, he was right. Our lives did return to normal for the next six months. Then all hell broke loose.

That was my first time inside a courtroom other than the short stint of fifteen minutes for my divorce, and once for an eviction proceeding for one of my tenants many years ago. This time, things were very different because this was so sudden. I had no idea what was about to occur. As the day wore on, I became more afraid than furious. My feelings were so intense that I wasn't sure of the magnitude of the fear until the moment I took a seat in the middle of the courtroom on the wooden bench. My legs were shaking uncontrollably.

The moments seemed to drag on. It felt as if I sat on that bench for hours before I caught a glimpse of my son. I watched in horror as my son shuffled in front of me dressed in a prison issue orange jumpsuit in handcuffs like a serial killer. A chain was attached to the handcuffs, which was attached to ankle cuffs. He shuffled along looking like a criminal walking in mud. The prison guard escorted him to stand before the judge. The judge's words sounded like they came from a *Peanuts* cartoon. Lucy, with her trumpet-like voice, was counseling Charlie Brown at her 5-cent psychiatrist's booth. It was all so surreal.

Although the charges would eventually be dismissed, I had no way of knowing that at the beginning of the arraignment. I thought a criminal charge would follow us forever. I envisioned us all with the dark cloud of the law hovering over us wherever we went in life.

What was real was that John's mind was no longer his own. But I thought he was just being reckless. I had no idea he was headed toward the abyss and nothing or no one could stop what was about to happen. My worst nightmare was coming true. Eventually, I would know the truth and be able to proceed accordingly with a diagnosis and treatment. I was horrified because, over the years, I had convinced myself that my son didn't carry the genetic predisposition of any mental illness. I admit that this thought had occurred to me many times in the past, but I surprised myself that I could even contemplate the words "mental illness." These words alone frightened me. I jumped back into reality when I heard my son's voice.

"Mom, thanks for getting me out. I am sorry for putting you through this. This will never happen again."

I wholeheartedly believed him, but only for a moment. The dropped charges didn't make everything disappear. My son's life would continue to unravel, and I would go down with him.

I had felt something big was about to happen after the arraignment and would have no control over it when it arrived. I had to finally push the thought aside and pass it off as the last little bit of fear rearing its head. Later that night, I fell fast asleep and slept for twelve hours. When I woke up the next morning, I convinced myself that John just got caught sowing his oats. He was drunk, lonely, and overworked in law school.

CHAPTER 9

MILAN

March 2005

EIGHT WEEKS BEFORE John was to graduate from law school, he called me on my cell phone. Hearing from him always lifted my heart. He was ready to graduate from law school, and I was so very proud of him. After all, this event was bigger than a graduation. It was about the family trait of being able to persist through determination. In modeling this trait, it was no surprise that my son would graduate law school at age twenty-three. He endured when he was tired. Chilling out was a rare thing for John. When he lost track, he would regroup, rethink, and go back to accomplishing his goals. Despite all the late nights studying or working part-time, practically all his successes were the result of his efforts and family support. He continued to outshine his peers scholastically. It was the hall-mark of his persistence through determination and the family environment. I took this personally. For me, his potential grad-uation also represented my own dreams that I'd held at bay until he was through with school. I often found myself sharing the good news about his upcoming graduation to anyone who would listen. I shouted it out to the whole world.

During that phone call, John told me he was at the airport leaving for Milan. He was difficult to understand on the phone.

He whispered or laughed between his words. He clearly wasn't himself. I was so preoccupied with his graduation in a couple of months, I didn't even think to ask why he was going and when he would return. All I could think about was who to invite to the celebratory lunch, how many hotel rooms to book, and activities for all. I was immersed in happiness at the thought of John finally graduating, and I had practically forgotten about his arraignment.

Within a week, James called me to tell me that John had missed his plane home and was stuck outside Milan. He was staying at the Waldorf Astoria. The private car, the hotel, and the airline ticket to New Orleans were two thousand eight hundred dollars, and John needed money. Something was very wrong. I became a nervous wreck during that phone call. John was so steady and rarely impulsive. Wait a minute! As I flashed upon the day trading and the arraignment incidents, I sensed that things were probably going to get worse.

I was totally humiliated and was not in any way able to pay for an unplanned plane ticket. I had to ask a friend for a thousand dollars. I had to hang onto what little I had, as I planned to continue my own education. It was on schedule as I had planned it. My joy was short-lived, however. My dream to pursue my PhD was soon to be, once again, elusive.

CHAPTER 10

THE ABYSS

April 2005

"Mrs. Denke, this is Mike Chamberlain from Medical Center of Louisiana emergency room in New Orleans."

It was around 4:30 p.m. and I was just about ready to leave work. I froze. I could no longer feel the beat of my heart or my own breathing. God only knew what the voice at the other end of the phone would say. I prepared myself for a loss from which I thought that I could never recover.

"I have your son John here in the emergency department. He was brought in by the police. It appears he is having a psychotic episode. The ED doctor has ordered medication, Risperdal Consta, bipolar medication. She admitted your son to the psychiatric unit. Has John ever heard voices or experienced hallucinations? Has he had any previous treatment for a mental illness?"

Thank God, my son was alive, and I was grateful. I had to shelve my emotions and use my adrenaline rush to form a plan. I rang my boss and told him that my son was admitted to the hospital in New Orleans for "exhaustion," and that I had to take some days off. I was unable to mouth the words "mental illness."

I couldn't believe for one minute that my son was ill and hospitalized, and, of all things, psychotic. Surely the caseworker was mistaken. I didn't even ask what precipitated his hospitalization.

I was overwhelmed. There was so much for me to do. While driving from Shreveport to New Orleans, I thought about what I would say to the law school administrators, Father Brown, and anyone else who had input about the fate of my son. How could this happen with six weeks left before he was to graduate? The trip to Milan preceded this event. All in all, he had missed almost three weeks from school.

All I could think of was John had gotten so far, and I was going to catch anyone who could influence the decision for him to graduate from law school. If it took meeting with the entire law school administration, I was prepared to do so. Yet I feared my mission could be stifled because of the enormous sigma that the words "mental illness" carried. Because of the embarrassment and shame I felt, I wished I could have called someone to help me with my emotions while driving to New Orleans, but my usual support systems were not an option for me. I couldn't disclose what had taken place with my son. So I did what any mother would do, I kept all my feelings inside. My goal was to do whatever I could to keep anyone from finding out that my son was diagnosed with bipolar disorder. My bias about mental illness looked me right in the eyes and I had to finally face the monster.

I arrived in New Orleans shortly after visiting hours were over. Psychiatric wards are known for their limited visiting hours even though regular hospitals have more relaxed visiting times. I was disappointed, but not with John. I was disappointed in everyone else who'd let John down, including God. I was *furious* with God. Hadn't my son been through enough? I knew one thing for sure; I would do everything humanly possible to be there for my son. One person is all it takes, and most of the time, one person is all you get.

I was so relieved that my son got back on track after the arraignment and was scheduled to graduate in May 2005. I reminded myself, and everyone else, of the date. As always, my heart jumped for joy at being so proud of my son. He called me less and less within that year, so I assumed that he was busy with his studies and exams. I was also busy planning for my own graduate studies. I was sure he was ecstatic about graduating from law school. We talked about it every time we spoke on the phone. I learned from that moment on never to assume anything.

I made it to the Holiday Inn Express, flung open the door of room 403, grabbed a handful of cashews and cranberries, and washed them down with a sip of room-temperature Diet Coke. I didn't even look at the sodium content. I stripped off my blouse and pants, then stepped into my Eileen Fischer nightgown. I finally fell into a deep sleep after worrying for hours.

In the morning, I filled the hotel coffee pot with tap water, opened a complimentary packet of regular Holiday Inn-issue coffee, and glanced at myself in the mirror. With a mouth full of cashews, I watched an image of myself in the mirror through salty tears streaming down my cheeks. My dreams for my son, and myself, shattered before my eyes. I prayed with desperation:

Our father, who art in Heaven, hallowed be thy name...
Please God, please return my son to sanity.

CHAPTER 11

MEDICAL CENTER OF LA

April 2005

MEDICAL CENTER OF Louisiana was a public teaching hospital. For New Orleans, the charity system was called the Medical Center of Louisiana at New Orleans (MCLNO), which included the iconic Charity Hospital (Big Charity), University Hospital, and affiliated clinics. MCLNO served a largely poor, uninsured population and accounted for eighty-three percent of inpatient and eighty-eight percent of outpatient uncompensated care costs in the New Orleans area in 2003.[1] It was also the dominant provider of psychiatric, substance abuse, and HIV/AIDS care in the region, and housed the lion's share of the region's inpatient mental health beds. Further, Charity Hospital was home to the Gulf Coast's only Level One trauma center and the busiest emergency department in the city. It served as the major teaching hospital both for the Tulane and LSU medical schools.

I could barely move from exhaustion when I walked into the hospital. Without any hint of what to expect, I imagined the worst. My son was in the psychiatric ward, which was unreachable by most. The thought of not being able to effectively communicate with a son whom I loved dearly was unfathomable.

This fact alone frightened me more than anything else I could imagine in life.

I was hypervigilant that morning. I observed my surroundings like a hawk after prey. When I stepped through the front doors, my eyes glanced around and felt the grandeur of the lobby. I imagined its luster a long time ago. I looked down at my feet at thick white marble floors, golden-flecked mortar, and rich Oriental rugs. The walls were shellacked a deep walnut color, as were the doorway entrances to other hallways and elevators. As I headed toward the information desk, I glanced at the overstuffed velour couches and chairs, which resembled the furniture from a manor home. This was a total contrast to what I had expected.

There were a couple of turn-of-the-century crimson velvet upholstered settees in the lobby, which were worn in places where visitors and patients sat over the years. There were other overstuffed couches and armchairs. Some of the floors and offices were newer and connected in the hallway. I saw the line of demarcation of the new and old building structures. Much of the building materials in the lobby were no longer used or were replaced by progress and cost.

Although the facility was dated, the lobby also resembled a grand hotel much like the Arlington Hotel in Hot Springs, Arkansas, with its white marble floors flecked with gold and black. The elevators were heavy, and looked like the old-time Otis elevators installed in most hospitals built during the early 1900s.

Throughout my nursing career, I had traveled extensively to conferences in the U.S. and internationally. I'd toured many a building and fell in love with art and architecture.

When I was pregnant with James, I became enamored with the pre-Civil War-era architecture and furnishings. I became a member of the National Preservation Historical Society.

My ex-husband and I walked through many museums, court-houses, stock exchanges, and hospitals built during this era, and they were similar in style and grandeur to the lobby of the Medical Center of LA. Although I enjoy architectural design and historic buildings, I was not in the mood that day, but I was grateful for the temporary diversion. That memory brought me some time before I had to face reality. I walked quickly past the grandeur, the concierge podium, and stepped into the elevator.

The psychiatric unit was on the ninth floor. I telephoned the hospital receptionist the night before I arrived at the hotel. She informed me of the visiting hours and the floor where my son was admitted. I purposely avoided the eyes of the other passengers, which was very unlike me. My face was red with shame. What was wrong with me?

I asked the man next to the elevator buttons to push floor nine for me. I suspected that everyone in the elevator knew the ninth floor was the psychiatric unit, and that I was going to visit my son there. I felt invisible because I was so tired of all that had happened and wondered why my life had turned out this way. I felt guilty that I was thinking only of myself, but when I am exhausted, I coalesce all the energy I can muster and focus on myself just to survive. My outlook on life was cloudy. I thought about my son and grieved for both of us. I didn't know how I was supposed to think or feel at that juncture.

The lack of energy, weariness, and negative outlook in life surely indicated that I might be depressed too. Would I need medication to cope with this? I certainly hoped not. We couldn't have two members in the family with mental disorders. Somebody had to hold up against this intense change in our lives. I couldn't get my head around what was happening. I feared that I couldn't cope with the grim reality of life then. How could I effectively deal? I realized that I measured my life from my own achievements and in the achievements of my sons. A diagnosis of mental illness felt disabling and weak. Although I often told my family and patients that mental illness is treatable, I didn't have faith in my own words because I wasn't entirely educated on the subject. I also bought into every stigma that our society has against mental illness. To what extent, I was soon to find out. My son's diagnosis conflicted with everything I held dear and valued. When I heard "mental illness," the words "weakness" and "guilt" and "homeless" immediately popped into my head. That didn't happen in my family. It wasn't going to happen to John.

My mind wandered, and my thoughts made no sense. My head spun, and I nearly fainted. My weariness, coupled with nausea, was frightening. I shifted my attention to more important issues. How in the world did my son end up in a psychiatric hospital? What did I miss? How did I miss the prodromal signs? Did I choose to deny the signs and ignore them? I beat myself to a pulp.

The lights in the elevator flashed above me. They blinked on and off as we stopped at the second, third, fourth, fifth, and the eighth floors. I stepped out of the elevator to make room for the people who wanted off. I was in the front of the car and a crowd stood behind me. I waited to hear someone behind me announce, "I'm getting out here," or "Excuse me," or push their way out without saying anything. I was claustrophobic, and aware of everything. We reached the ninth floor of the hospital. It took forever.

Father God, please be my guide now.

CHAPTER 12

NINTH FLOOR

How in the world had my son ended up in a psychiatric hospital? I wanted to be anywhere else but here. Anger and fear welled up within me, and I wondered why I couldn't command these feelings to disappear. Honestly, instead of having to face what was coming, I would have preferred to collapse in the elevator, hit my head, and never wake up.

Feeling paranoid, I was convinced everyone in the elevator knew my son was in the locked unit, or as we nurses called it, the "psych unit." My fear of anyone finding out about my son's diagnosis and admission was actively on my mind. It was my job to prevent that from happening.

My embarrassment was for me, not my son, and I didn't understand how I could feel that way. I realized I had despicable thoughts and feelings about mental illness and began to think about ways to deny it.

I didn't see any of my friends or colleagues wandering around the hospital, so a sense of relief rushed over me. My secret was safe. Once I visited my son and met with the doctors, I would have to craft a strategy to keep a lid on the real reason for my son's hospitalization. I desperately needed to keep this a secret.

Thinking about mental illness in my children did not make this fact go away. It was my role as a mother to figure out how to message this to everyone in my life. I was going drive myself crazy from the pressure of keeping secrets and making up lies. This was against everything I stood for. I never remembered having such intense feelings, and they frightened me. I was so close to panic then. If I could push aside my guilt and shame for feeling this way, I might be able to do whatever it took to maintain the secrecy. I simply wanted some control over my life again, and John's.

I realized I was selfish and thoughtless, thinking of myself first and foremost, and not my son at that point. My biases about mental illness were then so very clear to me, and I still jumped around in denial. I denied mental illness existed in my ex's family. No one in my family could ever be mentally ill. Rose, my ex's mother, was just eccentric. My ex was just an angry person. This kind of thing happened to *other* people. People with mental illnesses were wandering around the streets homeless, they didn't have working, functional lives like John. Surely the diagnosis was wrong. John must have fallen into a state of weakness with all his responsibilities. He would snap out of this. If there was something emotionally wrong with him, it was only temporary. This had to be my fault somehow.

I shook out of my depressed, dreamy state, pushed the button on the wall, and announced who I was and why I was there. One of the patient care techs scurried around the corner of the unit.

The lock to the entrance clicked, and the doors to the locked unit opened to the right side. I stepped in. The solid metal door slammed behind me. A second door clicked and swung open. Men and women were sitting at the nurse's station with their heads buried in their work or on their computers. An older man in his fifties, with a gold front tooth, smiled at me. I learned his name was Carlton. I smiled back at him, and he asked who I was there to see. I told him my name and that I was there to visit my son John.

I rambled on about how relieved I was that my son was in good hands, and how grateful I was to the police who brought him to the hospital. I told him that John was in the right place to receive treatment. I continued to share my nervous thoughts with Carlton, because I had no one else to talk to. So much had happened in the last couple of years that brought my son and me to that point.

I was anxious to talk to Doctor Fischer, the resident in charge of John's care. Carlton gave me her phone number so I could make an appointment to discuss John's diagnosis and treatment plan. I knew a family meeting was of the utmost importance. I had to be strong and focused. I had to fix it. But how?

I was the only member of my family present, just like many other meetings to come regarding my son. I strengthened myself inside, took a deep breath, and adjusted my facial expression to exude reassurance and steadiness for my son's sake. I was anxious, but not as much as I was when I first woke up that day.

John sat on the couch located to the side of the dayroom. That room was nothing more than an area outside of the patient rooms where almost everyone spent their daytime hours. John was thinner than when I had seen him last Christmas when he was home. His hospital issued pajamas hung on him. He appeared calm. He was most likely medicated, and for this, I was thankful.

John was coherent. We hugged tightly, said hello, and right away I noticed that his affect was flat, and his speech was quieter. I thanked God that he was at least safe for now. He was somewhat lucid but guarded.

John's hair was greasy and growing over his ears. He was always meticulous about his physical appearance, especially his hair. His legs were crossed, and he averted his eyes away from me as if my presence contributed to his inner anxiety. He looked at me with caution and suspicion. His eyes were glassy, and the lids hung over the upper third of his eye, almost like he was drunk or on street drugs. We sat squeezing each other's hands, talking very little. My son's eyes resembled the eyes of a dead patient who I had transported to the morgue during one of my evening shifts years ago. I wanted to wrap my arms around his state of mind so I could work this out for him.

A young girl with the same glassy eyes sat next to John. She had long, dark, stringy hair. She avoided eye contact with me. She seemed distant and secretive. I disliked her ignoring me and looking the other way when I spoke to her. Her presence caused my hair to stand on end, like when I have an intuitive flash of some kind or when I am feeling threatened in the presence of a person with bad vibes, although I observed nothing physical about her that alarmed me.

"Hi, I'm Linda, John's mother. How do you know John?"

She didn't answer. She was in her own world.

A nurse later stated that she was a regular at the hospital. She was discharged a week ago and was back on the day my son had arrived. Who was this girl? How could my son be so familiar with this girl I knew nothing about? Why was this bothering me so much?

Mark, John's roommate in the unit, ran up to me and almost knocked me over. He talked nonstop. His conversation was one-sided. He spoke rapidly and made little sense. He extended his hand while shifting back and forth on his feet. He asked me if I brought him a gift. I hesitantly shook his hand and told him I would give him the John Grisham book I had bought for John. I looked at Mark and saw his delight. I quickly made the decision to hand the book over to him. John was in his own world, and it seemed more appropriate to give it to Mark, rather than to John.

Quite frankly, besides my worry for John, I was disgusted about having to be in this position. Where had this uppity feeling come from? I'm a nurse. I'm John's advocate. As I stared at my son and the other patients milling around the unit, and that strange girl, an image from the film *One Flew Over the Cuckoo's Nest* came to mind. All I could think was my son playing the role of one of Jack Nicholson's sidekicks in the movie, an institutionalized psychiatric patient, a rule follower, lost in his own mind, his own world. This was not the life I had in mind for me or my son.

When I got to my hotel room, I realized that I didn't ask him what had happened. What happened that was so bad he ended up in a psych unit? I was still scrambling for a practical explanation, like an outside event, that had triggered his condition.

CHAPTER 13

DOCTOR FISCHER

DOCTOR ELIZABETH FISCHER was a young resident who was not much older than my son. She was in her thirties, petite in stature, with long, dark hair. I had called to schedule an appointment after I left the hospital. I arrived early and was ready to discuss the events that led to John's hospitalization. I was grateful for someone who cared about his condition. We walked to her makeshift office, a conference room.

As she shook my hand, she smiled and said, "Good afternoon, I'm Doctor Fischer, John's resident team leader during his hospitalization. I am a psychiatric resident. Neal, here, is my intern."

"I'm Neal. I'll be working with your son as well."

"It is nice to meet both of you. How can I help you help my son? How did John get here? He's is a wonderful son, and up until now, he was never a problem for either me or my ex-husband," I responded with trepidation.

Doctor Fischer spoke with great concern. "One of John's roommates called the police after witnessing an incident concerning a dog. Apparently the roommate walked to the backyard to get his dog and found that John was talking incoherently, tying the dog up with a garden hose. His roommate asked John to stop, but he wouldn't. He kept on talking as if he was in his own world. John didn't even acknowledge his friend.

His roommate called the police. The police report states that John was agitated and talking to himself all the way to the hospital. He was admitted to the psychiatric unit after about six hours in the ER. Has John ever been diagnosed with a mental disorder? Has he been treated? Has anyone on either side of the family been treated for bipolar disorder?"

Speechless and shocked, I began to tell her that John's grandmother was diagnosed with bipolar disorder and refused to take her medication. She was always noncompliant with her prescribed treatment. She didn't like how lithium made her feel. Although she received very little psychiatric care during my marriage, and was prescribed medications and other treatments, she did not follow through. Her husband simply gave up after years of trying desperately to support her with her follow-up treatment plans. After years of refusal to accept her illness, that repetitive cycle, and after his kids left home, he left too. She remained in her home until she became ill from a medical condition and died in her late eighties.

"My ex-husband exhibited bipolar behaviors, but he never acknowledged it. He was never on any medication, but should have been. His erratic behaviors were too much for me. Before we divorced, my attorney suggested he should be evaluated by a psychiatrist. He did do that, and the evaluation proved that he likely suffered from this disorder. The evaluation, and the need to protect my sons, launched the impetus for me to move ahead with the divorce. I was terrified to live my life following in the footsteps of my son's father. We divorced in 1985. I was somewhat frightened about the genetic predisposition in my husband's family. When my concerns were no longer unconscious, they began to fuel many of my decisions in my life regarding my children. I admit that I still care very much for my ex and keep watch over him like a helicopter parent who's never too far away. Funny as it seems, I didn't realize, or admit this fact until now," I confessed.

"Having a mother-in-law, an ex, or any loved one who was diagnosed with a serious mental illness and refused treatment is most devastating. I know what this feels like. I was a daughter-in-law and a wife, and the people I loved had a mental illness. I lived the experience of watching helplessly while they refused medication or any form of treatment. What is worse is standing by and not being able to do anything about it while trying desperately to deny they are mentally ill at all. All the money and access to providers and healthcare in the world cannot make someone you love seek treatment, or when they finally decide to do so, it is unknown whether this individual will comply with the treatment. I understand there are many reasons for noncompliance, but mostly I now understand some of this stems from the lack of acceptance of the fact that you must own your mental illness. Other reasons are the side effects from the medications which can include enormous weight gain, changes in personality, a more controlled lifestyle to the point of boredom, and the stigma surrounding how others see the illness."

Doctor Fischer and Neil listened intently and wrote notes while I told my story.

"John said that he wants to go home and finish law school. Do you have any thoughts about this plan?" I wanted to know.

Doctor Fischer expressed concern. "I believe that if John responds positively to the first line treatment of medications, it will be possible. He'll require supervision for a short time, a stable environment, and support to finish school. Afterward, the plan will be up to John."

"Since my son wants to finish school and take his exams, do you think he can be discharged by the end of this week?" I pleaded. "I want to meet with the school administration and see what arrangements can be made for John to stay in a secure environment, study, and pass his exams so he can graduate as planned. He said he wanted to get out of the hospital and he's tasked me with whatever I could do to make that happen. He said he will be forever grateful."

"Possibly, yes, I agree. We will plan for aftercare, and by Monday we will draw John's labs and plan for his discharge," she replied with enthusiasm.

"Great! John will be released on Monday? I know that his life will change forever. I am new to all of this, even though I am a nurse. This treatment and care is unfamiliar to me, but I will do whatever possible to support John in every way. This happened so suddenly, I am unable to think too far ahead into the future right now. What is my son prescribed?"

"John is on a first line treatment medication for his condition, but I want to stabilize him before I discharge him," Doctor Fischer answered. "We can draw his labs a few days before his discharge."

Not only was my life not only not my own anymore, but my son was now dependent on mood stabilizers and other unknown antipsychotic medications, perhaps for the rest of his life. While I knew from my training that medication choices were limited, I was willing to follow the advice of the physician who diagnosed and prescribed them to my son. The combinations of a mood stabilizer and antipsychotic medications were necessary to stabilize him and keep him that way.

She made notes, and I told her that I was committed to do whatever necessary to get John back into law school as soon as possible, and somehow make sure he would take his medications. I wondered if the first line of treatment included lithium.

I can remember fading out from our conversation into a pleasant memory. John, James, and I were on vacation in Hot Springs, Arkansas, playing in the steam that floated off the surface of the outdoor pool. We splashed one another and free-floated on our backs. Later, in the lobby, I stopped to drink some natural spring water, supposedly filled with super health benefits. I could see the little sign above the fountain: *The list of healthy ingredients contained in this spring water include carbonates, bicarbonates of magnesium, sodium, potassium, calcium and lithium.* Lithium? That vacation proved that we were a happy, healthy, stable family. It had nothing to do with the natural lithium in the water.

Our Father who art in Heaven, please guide me in the right direction to help John.

CHAPTER 14

A MIRACLE

LOYOLA UNIVERSITY NEW Orleans College of Law is the place where my son suffered the most in his life. All I could think about was that John had gotten this far, and I was going to see to it that anyone who could influence the decision for him to graduate would be my target.

My plan was to meet with Associate Dean, Susan Bouive, first. On my drive there, one thing reverberated in my mind. I was going to do anything I could to fulfill John's wish to graduate. My son needed an advocate. I would do anything for him to get him better. I kept thinking about this until I screamed it out loud in the car for what seemed like miles.

Dean Bouive was a matter-of-fact woman around fifty, silver blonde hair, athletic, and small. Her demeanor paved a clear path for the conversation about my son. She spoke highly of John and was aware of his potential success due to his grades and performance. We talked about the classes John had missed, and the possibilities to secure new living arrangements for him. She told me to excuse her for a moment so she could make a call to Father Brown. After her conversation, she directed me to his office down the hall for a meeting with him. I was going to have a face to face with him and wasn't sure what to expect.

Father Brown appeared right on schedule for our 11:00 a.m. meeting. He was about five foot ten, silver haired, around seventy, and looked exactly like a typical Catholic priest. A Catholic priest reminds me of a Santa-like man wrapped in black cloth who displays a blend of stoic and soft personality traits. They always seem to know exactly what to say. Catholic priests are pivotal persons upon whom I rely heavily in my times of crisis. Not once had any of the priests I had ever sat in front of or confessed to ever failed to possess all the right answers for life's dilemmas. This meeting guaranteed me a moment to relax and would ease my troubles about my son... for a short while.

I sat down in front of Father Brown's long mahogany desk. As I did, I glanced at the top of his desk and saw a shiny silver desk pen holder. An engraved silver pen was etched with the words, "Father Brown for your continued service." A leather-like desk board and several framed diplomas dating back to 1988 lined the wall, indicating his tenure at the law school to be just shy of twenty years then.

Father Brown's face had a look of concern. I guess he knew that John was accepted into law school at twenty-one years of age and started right after he turned twenty-two years of age. At twenty-one, John was legally able to drink and vote, but his friends were in their late twenties and early thirties, with more life experiences than John.

Father Brown looked at me with compassion as I spilled my guts about the events leading up John's hospitalization. I struggled to speak the words "bipolar disorder" and instead, the words "depression, stress, and exhaustion" came out of my mouth. He unfolded his aged hands as I looked at him through my tears. Disclosure was not something with which I was comfortable. I was a private person.

Private? Yes! I had to keep a secret!

I desperately longed for some relief from the grief of this burden. I realized seeing my child locked away in a psychiatric hospital was traumatic for me. I too was locked inside a psychiatric unit, isolated and untouchable. I remained ever present with John long after I left the ward.

After I saw my son in the state he was in, I was furious with God. I always relied on God and my faith, and at that moment, I wavered. I was overwhelmed with grief and sorrow at the thought of my son and his fate. I felt so helpless.

The day had just begun and I was already overwhelmed with the treatment plan and what the future would hold for me and my son, let alone his career and my family. I was paranoid about what the students and the professors would think about my son and me. I truly hoped that nobody would find about John's breakdown.

Please, don't let his teachers find out!

I simply asked Father Brown for his assistance in finding some way John could return to school and take the necessary steps to graduate. Father Brown, along with Dean Bouive, set into play a series of steps that allowed my son to return and graduate on time. What he arranged was nothing short of miraculous. When he was discussing his plans for John to finish law school, I was immersed in my own fears and thoughts. That was the first time I'd told anyone about John's hospitalization. During the meeting with Father Brown, feelings of embarrassment barged their way in. I was ashamed of my mother-in-law, my ex, and I was becoming embarrassed about John's condition. The words "John" and "mental illness" didn't belong in the same sentence. They were not one and the same. My bias about mental illness was deep-seated, but I had no idea where my perceptions were housed within me. I was becoming great at denying that issue, and at the same time, my denial was weakening. I had enough guilt and shame because I felt somehow responsible for John's condition, so I used denial to the point where it could no longer work. I didn't have any energy to explore my bias. Besides, nobody knew about these feelings. I suffered in silence behind my wall while I'd cared for my mother-in-law and my ex, and now I was caring for John. I was John's mother, and I cared about his health, welfare, and well-being. I cared about his safety. I still carried hope that the doctors had misdiagnosed him. Surely he'd just broken down from exhaustion. I couldn't grasp that my son was suffering from bipolar disorder. It wasn't possible. But was it? My thoughts were like a yo-yo.

Father Brown gave me the directions to a convent. This was where and when I understood what Dean Bouive and Father Brown's plan was nothing less than a miracle.

$$\text{OOO}$$

Sister Sophia was glad to help. She assured me that she would escort John to the wrought iron gate every morning, and she would be there upon his return in the afternoon. She promised to take good care of him. She took me to his room. It was a basic room, and it had a peaceful feel to it, as if it had been blessed. The bed was tiny with just one flat pillow at the head. A brown wool blanket was perfectly tucked under the mattress. An antique chest of drawers sat in a dark corner, and the small desk could be unlocked with an ancient-looking key. I gave her my contact information in case she needed to call me for any reason.

Mad at God and feeling sorry for myself, I walked to my car, crying all the way. Yet in this place of peace, I experienced a huge sense of relief. I felt wrapped in a womb, safe and content, pleased and satisfied. My son was going to finish law school and graduate. John was strong and resilient, and I thought he would be fine. I truly believed he would fully recover after he was discharged from the hospital. Perhaps he might get to a point to where he no longer needed medication. Maybe?

Sister Sophia did take good care of John, and he did finish law school.

Our Father, who are in Heaven…thank you for this miracle and all your blessings.

OOO

My son was named after John Paul, who was the first non-Italian pope after centuries at the time of John's birth. My prayers began fervently when he was diagnosed. My prayers went to my son's patron saint, John Paul, and directly to God. My own suffering resonated with the suffering that John Paul experienced for himself and his people when he was a young man growing up in Poland. He watched the invasion of his country by the Nazis during WWII. He represented hope and love in a time of great suffering and genocide of the Polish people. He survived with a great understanding of suffering and grief. Because of his faith in God, he exuded love and hope throughout the world during his papacy. I know that the miracles I experienced during John's suffering and his eventual return to health was a miracle. I know my prayers helped my own pain as a mother of a troubled son. He helped me get through my own shame, hopelessness, and the sigma that comes with mental illness.

John Paul, please watch over John. Take him into your loving heart.

CHAPTER 15

CLUES

I WENT TO John's old apartment after I left the convent. I told his roommate, J.B., that I needed to pick up my son's belongings. J.B. looked at me devoid of any empathy or understanding, mumbling that his grandfather wasn't going to be very happy now that John wasn't coming back since he paid his rent each month. I just stared at him with disdain, pulled out my checkbook, and wrote him a check for half the month's rent. I told him I would mail him the rest at the end of the month. He failed to say thank you, kiss my ass, or anything. I was grateful when he left the room. I never saw or spoke to him again.

I stared at the complete disaster that was my son's room. I always knew him to be neat and overly tidy. He used to compartmentalize his socks and hung his shirts by color and style. This was no longer the case, and I was quite surprised that he could be this messy. Was this what his mind looked like?

I found a postcard crumpled up in a pile of papers, pens, pencils, and various other school supplies. His bed was unmade, and his sheets were laying on the floor as if he were sleeping on them instead underneath them. Where was his pillow?

I stripped the bed, gathered the sheets, and picked up the garbage. I saw a tape recorder with a tape in it. I was curious, but afraid to hear what was on the tape. I turned it on anyway. I heard whispered words, muffled but audible, of lewd and licentious phrases. There were irrational but recognizable curse words coming out of the mouth of my son. John always had made it a point to avoid curse words at all costs. He truly believed that it was distasteful to curse. I was shocked and confused. My hands trembled and fumbled while I attempted to turn off the recorder, tears streaming from my eyes. I collapsed into a squatting position, and then curled into a fetal position. My heart broke and my dreams for my son's future evaporated. I let out all my feelings and cried until I could cry no more. I could care less who heard me.

How could things get this bad?

I sat up and saw a pile of papers in the corner near the wastebasket. It seemed strange to me that the pile of checking account statements, electric bills, old envelopes, and convenience stores receipts were crumbled up in the pile alongside the garbage, not in it. I opened each one carefully so I would not miss anything important like a bill that needed to be paid or anything that might be overdue.

One bank statement seemed unusually thick. I unfolded the statement, which contained eleven pages of items and was dated February–March 2005. Much to my surprise, I counted a string of thirty-eight ATM withdrawals from 3:16 a.m. until 4:51 a.m. Each withdrawal was for as little as one dollar or as much as twenty dollars. By the twentieth withdrawal, all the money was gone, and further attempts to withdraw money were declined.

One by one, I opened receipts for cigarettes, Cheetos, ham sandwiches, and dental floss. A rush of sadness came over me, but I vowed not to cry anymore that day. As I gathered myself and stood, I saw a shiny piece of crumpled paper near the garbage. It was separate from the finished pile in my son's room that I had already gone through. I reached for the paper and opened a glossy postcard from the Ritz Carlton in Milan, Italy. On the back was a handwritten note that read:

Baglioni Hotel Carlton Staff
Via Senato, 5, 20121 Milano MI, Italy

Dear John,

The staff at the Ritz Carlton want to say thank you for staying with us in Milano. Please come to visit us anytime. We look forward to it!

It felt like I was moving in slow motion. John's apartment was in an old quaint home off St. Charles Avenue. It was a typical old New Orleans home with a wraparound front porch, large balcony, and hardwood floors. His bedroom was on the second floor. I continued to pack my son's belongings into a thirty-gallon trash bag. My whole life at that instant seemed unreal. The fact was, I was in my son's apartment for three hours. I sorted through papers, school supplies, bed sheets, closets, and piles of clothes that were strewn across his bed and bedroom floor, and everywhere else outside his bedroom door. The heaviness of this realization weighed me down. I was ashamed and sad that my son was scrounging around for money, which was a common theme that ran through our lives in those days, feeling poor and broke.

I was surrounded by chaos and, I was sure, tons of germs. I guessed he hadn't cleaned his room for as long as he had lived there. Dust was everywhere. I uncovered large spots of mold and the stench was unbearable. I began to feel like a leper, as if I had a contagious disease and were living in a leper colony. I began to understand the emotional aspect of the stigma of mental illness. I understood that cultures needed normal models of human behavior. I understood that any deviation from "normal" thinking is disturbing and disgusting for many. Mental illness was and is so very misunderstood. I was feeling what John must have felt, although I wasn't sick. I still felt the weight of the age-old wrong thinking that we all experience at one time or another in our lives.

All my son's clothes in his closet were carefully folded and placed in a plastic bag. As I scanned the bedroom one last time, I spotted a heavy, vinyl, yellow and light gray winter coat I did not recognize. It was folded up on the floor toward the back of John's closet. I didn't remember this jacket and I was certain I hadn't bought it for him. Since it was in the room, it must have been his. I reached to pick up the coat. The jacket was stiff and heavy and difficult to fold. It was made of an unfamiliar material. It probably weighed over five pounds. I focused on the jacket like a laser when I saw gray block letters written across the back of the jacket. To my surprise, the word "POLIZIA" appeared before my eyes. The lapel of the jacket folded open and I saw a second set of smaller block letters with the word, "MILANO" Panic electrified me as questions flooded my mind.

Our Father, who art in Heaven, hallowed be thy name. Please guide me to the right place in my heart and mind to help you help my son.

CHAPTER 16

DO NO HARM

I WAS BEGINNING to understand that a diagnosis of bipolar illness brought a whole world of stigma. And with any stigma, there is exclusion in every way. The hell with all this talk about inclusion. I learned that the majority of my friends really didn't understand mental illness, and most of my friends were *nurses*. Come to think of it, *I* knew very little about it. It never occurred to me that this illness would visit my son and stay. A couple of times, when I did share my feelings, I regretted it, so I talked about the stress of law school and finance when they asked about John. I refrained from reaching out to them, except Catherine.

Catherine was my dear friend in graduate school, and she appeared in my life in 2006. Although this was one year after my son's diagnosis, I did not share any of my sons journey though his mental illness and his difficulties adjusting with anyone up until Catherine.

Catherine was my closest friend. This nightmare of my son's journey through his mental illness for me, did not escape me, nor was his journey shared by me with another until 2006, when I finally had to find solace in another human being. I began to slowly trust again and Catherine helped as this story slowly leaked out of me and reveal the real me, more and more as we became closer and our friendship deepened. The pain inside me had become to great not to let go and Catherine provided the impetus for me to finally share my heart ache about my son's and his mental illness with another compassionate human being.

She listened and offered support, which is what I needed, to be accepted, not judged. I shared the ugly stigma of the diagnosis as it crept into me and my daily world. She helped me understand the isolation that other mothers must feel when their child is diagnosed with mental illness. I know I was isolated, but I had the same stigmatic attitudes that I thought only others had. If I lied to myself and denied my biases, I could keep believing that there could be a better life for us once we got past this crisis. I had to deny all my feelings so I could support John. This was the worst thing that I could have done for both of us. It kept me at a distance. The tiny bit of education that I received in nursing school depicted images of mentally ill patients in the extreme. That information was dated. The images on film to educate us were horrific. It depicted an illness that I thought was unmanageable. I didn't want any part of becoming a psychiatric nurse. If I'd only known then what I know now.

I was desperate, and I longed for a life of my own. I wanted to escape this situation for good. I couldn't see that the relationship between my judgements regarding mental illnesses and my desire to run was really a desire to escape my intense feelings. It really had nothing to do with John's condition. Thankfully, I would soon understand that all the intensity was directed at myself, not at John and his condition.

I kept silent and receded into the background. As I lived through another bad experience, I braced myself to feel a stab in the heart. Little by little, my denial diminished as I became aware of the fact my son suffers from bipolar disorder. He slips into another world. I wondered if my own wounds would ever heal. I would beat myself up, get out my computer, and add up all my failed attempts to heal all of us. I found myself deciding to give up and run away. I meant it at the time. But I would open my eyes and instantly jolt back into the present. I realized that I was living in a nightmare. My beloved son John was surrounded by darkness. This darkness surrounded not only him, but also, me. This darkness resembled an eclipse as the moon moves across the sky and covers the sun. Light one minute, dark the next. The brilliance faded. His sunlit aura was nonexistent. I feared his light will be blocked and darkness would replace his luster forever.

As a mother, I wanted to do everything in my power to keep my children out of harm's way. I realized that I might have failed miserably as a mother. I wanted to run away when I looked at John. I felt so helpless. As a nurse, I was taught to be aware of my values and to refrain from making any judgments about my patients. Feelings of judgement and righteousness shocked me. I owned my poor performance as a mother. Despite my knowledge of genetics, guilt and shame were rampant. Deep inside myself, I believed *I* was the cause of my son's bipolar disorder. It took me many years to find the support I needed to realize I wasn't responsible. I really didn't cause John's illness.

My feelings of helplessness soon turned into anger. This anger was no stranger to me. I often become angry when I feel confused and frightened. The first time I experienced an overwhelming feeling of fear as an adult was one of the many times when my mother warned me about mental illness and genetics. It was after I'd gotten married and I was around my mother-in-law much more than when David and I were engaged. Nevertheless, I *had* made the decision to marry into a family with a genetic predisposition to bipolar disorder and have children within that marriage. On a rational level, I knew that any child of mine would likely carry the genes for this condition.

Lost within my excitement, I expected that I would have a perfectly healthy family, and it was likely that this trait would skip a generation or not show up at all.

Condensing my past, I had no idea that darker days would lie ahead for John after he left law school. If I had known what was going to take place inside his brain, I would have done anything in my power that I could to prevent this from happening in his life. John became a shadow of himself. I couldn't have predicted what was to take place inside his mind. No one could. The shadow that would soon surround him would drown out the light from his sunlit aura. My memories of his young presence reminded me of the warmth from the sun during the long-ago summer days when my family vacationed at the beach. John loved the beach. I could still see him when he was a child, laughing and happy in his brilliant light. That memory continually sustains me.

The events that took place within the next couple of years were so tragic. No one could convince me that my beloved son, the child I loved with all my heart, could have landed in the Orleans Parish Prison, fade into oblivion, and end up in a psychiatric hospital. The deterioration of his mind caused physical deterioration, trouble in school, bruised relationships, erratic behaviors, avoidance of responsibilities, and ruined hopes and dreams. John slowly and steadily began to fade during the next few years. The son I knew and loved eventually vanished. He was lost. I was lost.

The symptoms, the clues, and the explosion were only the tip of the iceberg. A combination of genetics, stress, substance abuse, and more were the very triggers that snatched my son's rationality and replaced it with an unpredictable and irrational mind. My familiar world disappeared, and disappointment reared its head, landed inside my heart, and crushed me.

To watch someone you love mentally slip away from reality, day after day, without any ability to stop the process, is one of the most helpless feelings a mother can experience, especially when the someone slipping away is your child.

No matter what I must do, or however long it takes, I will find you, John.

CHAPTER 17

HOME

May 2005

THIS VISIT TO see my son in the hospital awakened me to the grim reality that my son was diagnosed with a mental illness, but I still had a shred of hope that he was simply exhausted. That hope began to slip away as his behavior became more erratic and strange. How would he manage? How would my family manage? My biggest fear was that I wouldn't be able to communicate with him ever again.

John returned to class and finished final exams. With the assistance of Sister Sophia, his professors, and Father Brown, John graduated from law school. There was no celebration. There were no guests, no caps thrown into the air, and no luncheon. In May 2005, John's law school diploma found its way to his home. Simultaneously, so did the hospital bill from John's initial hospitalization from April 1, 2005, until April 12, 2005, for 17,409.70 dollars. I was shocked.

Once again, my children were keeping me in a state of poverty-like existence. I was consumed with many attempts to keep my head above water. My existence, hopes, and dreams were fading away.

When bipolar disorder is untreated, the condition behaves like any other untreated illness. The individual's mental and physical health is affected, and because of this deterioration, the family deteriorates as well. The thought of losing someone I love, who was still physically healthy, with no understanding of how his behavior was controlled by his sick brain, was unbearable. One year after his diagnosis, a combination of studying for the law license exam, a potential law position, and structuring his life while living with me provided the stability John required to pass the exam. Some days he was near normal. Other days he suffered, so I hung onto his good days. I began to feel that over the next year and a half, he could return to normalcy. When I received a letter of acceptance into the PhD program at the University of Texas at Arlington, I was ecstatic and my family was joyful. Classes started in spring 2006. Since John seemed stable, I began preparations to start graduate courses as planned.

Unfortunately, drinking, stress, and a weakened physical condition combined to form the perfect storm. The final trigger was when John stopped taking his medications. Within one year after passing the bar and landing an associate position in a law firm, in the middle of the night John left my house. He took all his belongings with him. The only item left in his nightstand drawer was a half a bottle of lithium. This was the first time he stopped taking his medications, therefore the delusions and voices returned. He went directly to his father's house without any explanation.

Our Father...please let him be safe at David's house now that I can't be there twenty-four/seven.

CHAPTER 18

NEW YORK

2006

JOHN STAYED AT his father's house for only two months, then he was off to a potential law position in New York. For the life of me, I couldn't figure out why he was going there. He never told me or David that he was even applying for a job. I thought our lives were becoming more manageable when he lived with me after his discharge from the Medical Center of LA. But I was so wrong.

When John first left, I couldn't calm down or sleep. I felt like I was losing my mind. I was exhausted every day. Thank God he called me on a regular basis and sounded sane, stable, and calm. I was surprised and relieved, so I eventually calmed down as well.

My mother and I planned a trip to New York to attend the theatre months before John left. I called John and invited him to dinner with my mother and me after we arrived in New York City. When we walked out of the theatre, I checked my messages. David had called me with panic in his voice yelling at me to call him immediately. He told me that John was in Christ Hospital's emergency department in Jersey City. John's landlord had called David to inform him that John was acting strange and had thrown his computer out the window onto the sidewalk. The landlord had called 911, and David had informed the physicians at the hospital about John's condition and history. John had had another psychotic episode.

When John was discharged, my mother and I took the bus back to Pennsylvania where my mother lived. John needed a few days to stabilize, so he stayed with her until David and James drove in from Dallas to pick him up and take him back home to live with his father. My mother would make sure he took his medication until he left for Dallas. He was given a prescription for Geodon at the hospital with strict instructions on how and when he should take it. I was due back to work so I caught a flight back to Dallas feeling relieved that John was in good hands.

While my mother was waiting for David and James to arrive, John began to unravel. When I called her to check on him after I returned home, she said that he seemed much more agitated. At 3:00 a.m. the next morning she was awakened by the clinking of glass coming from her sitting room. When she got downstairs to check it out, she found John rummaging through the liquor cabinet and attempting to pour himself a bourbon and Coke. He ignored her pleas to stop. She tried to tell him that it would only make matters worse. She called me at 7:00 a.m., frantic because of John's increasing agitation and inability to sleep. It didn't occur to us at the time that the Geodon wasn't working as we expected, or that it had even had time to work. The physician at the hospital didn't inform us of these much-needed details. (This information, or lack thereof, happened more than once.) I did my best to reassure my mother that David would be there that afternoon to pick him up. She did her best to calm down. I'm sure she was terrified. I was ready to give up on John for making my mother feel that way. The mere thought of letting all of this chaos go once and for all made me feel lighter. But again, the heaviness of it all grabbed me like a ball and chain, and I couldn't be free. It didn't occur to me that the ball and chain was there because I put it there. I would find out about that much later during his last hospitalization.

By the time John got back to Dallas, he was in a psychotic state again.

CHAPTER 19

LOST

March 2007

I REMEMBER THE day David called me told me that John had left the night before and didn't return home. I was flabbergasted. After New York, he was up and down, but less intense. David told me that since John wasn't taking his medications and had no job, he had said to him, "It's my way or the highway." John chose the highway.

My ex and I weren't on the same page about how to raise our sons. Actually, we weren't on the same page about many things, yet we came together on making the tough decision to let John go and allow him to hit "rock bottom." This "tough love" approach horrified others, and I waffled with this decision every hour. John was in denial; he refused to take his medications. He walked out on his job, one he'd secured a few weeks after David picked him up from my mother's house. I was emotionally and financially drained. I could barely support myself. Between trying to go to work daily, and my intense worry about his diagnosis, I was losing it too. After years of living under these conditions, I had no other alternative but to let John go. I had nothing left to give. I put John in God's hands. I held him in my heart and tried to forgive myself.

I wrestled with the decision to call the police to report him as missing, but something kept me from doing so. After four days, we got a call from the day shift manager of the Days Inn in Plano, Texas. He notified us that John had left the motel without paying the bill. At least we knew after four days of him being missing John was alive. We didn't pay the motel bill.

During the months after John went missing, I would receive an occasional phone call from the police telling me they had picked him up in various towns. The police would always tell me that they felt that John belonged to someone since he was so articulate and just didn't fit the profile of a homeless person. I reluctantly informed them of John's condition, that he refused to take his meds, that he was noncompliant regarding treatment, and that we were at our wit's end emotionally, as well as financially spent. The officers understood and would inform us where they were going to take him. Usually it was to a hospital or a homeless shelter. These calls assured us that he was alive and somewhat determined his location. While this gave me a little comfort, we didn't get a call every day.

On one occasion, I got a call from the mother of an old college friend of John's, Adam. His mother told John that he could stay at her house if he had no place to go. She offered to take him to a hospital, but he declined. He found out that someone he barely knew was living in Miami, so he went back on the road and headed to Florida with the intention to see her. He hitch-hiked to Miami, catching rides from sketchy people or strange truck drivers. Eventually, a kind person gave him one hundred dollars and took him to the bus station.

On his way to Florida, I received a call from a nurse in the emergency room in Opelika, Alabama. It was determined that John was psychotic. I almost had a breakdown at that. Despite my better judgement, I made the decision to immediately drive to Alabama to retrieve him. The good news was that John was safe and being cared for. The bad news was that before I got off the phone with the nurse, John left against medical advice. Once he got to Aventura, a small town outside of Miami, he made his home in a mall parking lot. He slept there and got food from the food court out of garbage cans or what was left on the trays. I learned later that John was arrested trying to steal a pair of pants from Kmart. Strangely, I was relieved he wasn't in jail. At least he had food to eat and a bed on which to sleep.

We received the last call about John in the middle of the night. Officer Johnson informed us that John was almost hit by a truck driver right outside Miami. He was walking in the middle of the highway. They took him to the emergency room in Aventura. This was his fifth emergency room hospitalization in five different states since he left. It was his third inpatient hospitalization since he had been diagnosed.

After John returned home and was lucid, we plotted his route as he walked or hitchhiked from Texas to Florida. Remarkably, he could recall every highway and every exit while he was lost. We determined he covered a total of 1,313.90 miles.

CHAPTER 20

FOUND

April 2007

SINCE 2005, John's illness has taken a toll on my family and me. Why? Because he was noncompliant with taking his meds and with his treatment plan. Our lives had become unmanageable. John's illness wreaked havoc on my finances too. The most difficult period for me was when I realized my hopes and dreams for my son were in jeopardy. All the plans I envisioned for him after law school evaporated.

A nervous breakdown seemed imminent. I wanted it to happen just to get it over with. For all kinds of reasons, I assumed responsibility for the chaos and damage. Simply stated, I am John's mother and a mother protects her child from harm despite the sacrifice to her own well-being. This is an unrealistic expectation for any mother. When his illness struck, I felt helpless and inept because there was nothing I could do to keep the illness from snatching my son. There are no words to describe the pit of hollowness in my heart.

I realized there was no reprieve from the fact that my son was there one moment and gone the next. I was unsure about how to feel, or where to turn. My mind required constant redirection to stay focused on the present. When John went missing, I was alone and frightened. I struggled to deflect thoughts about my son and his whereabouts, but I was obsessed about it. Time stood still. I couldn't talk to anyone, and my emotions spilled over into everything I did. I receded into the background of life. No more sharing. I decided to keep my shock and disbelief to myself. One day out of the blue, my professor asked me if I was keeping a secret and if everything was okay. I suppose I wasn't hiding my pain that well.

At that juncture, I decided to take a back seat and disengage from the joy in life, probably to punish myself. Now I cannot imagine why I chose this path, yet at the time, that choice made sense to me. While John was sick, I immersed myself in my full-time doctoral coursework and worked at the University of Texas at Arlington as a graduate associate for the nursing school I was enrolled. If I didn't, a mental breakdown was unavoidable.

Honestly, since my goal was to finish my degree, I was hopeful from time to time. I thought that finishing my degree would affirm that I still had a bit of sanity and could somewhat function in the world. Although I felt worthless as a mother maybe I could do *something* right.

○○○

When I walked into your room at Aventura Hospital, my heart felt like it was slowly breaking. I smiled and walked slowly over to you, frightened not to do anything that would scare you. As soon as I saw you I knew you would never be the same. Your mind seemed slower than I remember, and of course, that was a side effect of the many medications they gave you. You were dressed in hospital-issued pajamas and were as thin as the scarecrow in The Wizard of Oz.

I didn't know how to behave. I was uncertain about how you would react, so I moved closer and gave you a gentle hug. I was terrified and relieved at the same time and stopped myself from doing anything that might frighten you. I felt so helpless that you had to go through this experience alone. Yet I was thankful that you did because I could tell, as soon as I saw you, that you had made the decision to stand up to your illness. You were spent. I knew that you would never be the same, but I had no earthly idea of how this would manifest. The sight of you in the hospital bed made me realize how precious you are to me.

I noticed when you crossed your leg that you had two open wounds the size of fists on the back of both of your heels. Your hair was long and greasy. On the bedside table, I noticed the sharp contrast of dirty dental floss and a clean toothbrush. I was happy that you still took the time to physically care for yourself.

The police said they found you in the middle of a major highway and a truck driver notified them after he swerved out of the way not to hit you. The driver was so shaken after the experience that he notified the police. He got out of his truck and convinced you to wait with him for the police to arrive. After a few minutes of talking to you, the police took you to the nearest hospital.

○○○

I thank God for The Baker Act[2]. In Florida, The Baker Act gives the police the authority to take anyone with a diagnosable mental illness to a psychiatric facility for treatment for seventy-two hours. This one law and the Miami police officers saved his life.

As we were preparing to leave, the nurse who oversaw the unit asked John to promise to always continue with his medication. John said that he would, and he continues to do so to this day. But this was not the happy ending at all.

Father God, thank you for guiding John to safety. Thank you for this miracle.

Give me the patience and guide me to the next step to take from here.

CHAPTER 21

HOME AGAIN

April 2007

MY PLAN WAS to take John back to my home where he could be safe. The road trip to Dallas was going to be about twenty-two hours. I rented a car in Miami, and then I gathered John, his medications, treatment plan, and drove as fast as I could from the hospital back to Dallas. Since he was so thin, I planned to stop at fast food restaurants to get him started on a weight-gain plan. I couldn't think of healthy food at that point. I would tend to that when we got home.

John's mental and physical condition continued to disturb me. As a nurse, the open wounds on his heels were my greatest concern because of a risk for infection. As a mother, I continued to blame myself for his mental condition and even his physical problems. The hospital decided to simply allow the open wounds to heal on their own. No dressing, no antibiotic ointment, nor salve of any kind was ordered. Therefore, I took it upon myself to nurse my son to health.

The wounds began to heal. I obsessed and inspected the wounds every twenty-four hours, if not more often. John was skin and bones. I was bound and determined to take matters into my own hands and move him into David's home as we'd both agreed. I was working part-time at the University of Texas at Arlington and attending full-time graduate school. David wasn't working at all. But I still had to micromanage John's health and medications and advise David what to do to care for him. I planned to spend as much time with him as I could and visit him every day.

OOO

As the days wore on, all I could see in John's eyes was a distant expression with only a rare glimpse of joy that I recognized as the person who "once was" John, the one who had disappeared, gone forever. I prayed this was just a bad dream. It was like I was living in two distinct realities. One was tangible, happening in front of me, and the other was invisible, where I could only guess what was going on with John because he responded to things so differently than anyone else.

One minute I got lost trying to interpret John's emotions and words, the next, my interpretations were ridiculously off base. Sometimes he was logical, and I would trick myself into a false state of being hopeful; other times I would just give up. This became a game I played in my head each day while I scurried around the house doing chores on the weekends when he stayed with me. My job as a nurse became a respite of sorts outside the home.

I couldn't escape the sorrow that resulted from watching the colossal changes inside John's entire being as he slipped away from me, hoping against hope that somebody would prevent these changes from happening. While I knew I had to get my arms around the fact that there was nothing I could do to stop his illness, I couldn't at that point. I couldn't give up on trying the impossible. I kept vigil, and went through the motions of making certain he was okay and took his meds. Although I tried to give him a sense of normalcy on a day-to-day basis, nothing since the breakdown was normal. Pretending became a way of life. That slow, methodical dance was essential and necessary just to survive. I could never visit with John in his mind, so I found myself desperately attempting to get his attention to fish for a word or response that would take me back to the way he used to be. Someone with this illness doesn't physically die but their minds are arrested and the chatter in their heads can only be understood by them.

Then the voices began. Rarely did John's conversations include me. Mostly he would converse with other people who lived inside his mind.

One, two, three, four voices gradually surfaced within John. It scared me almost to the point of sheer panic when he talked back to them. To this day, John can remember and describe the voices. Each individual voice had a tone and cadence of its own. Each voice had something unique to say to him, and he had his unique way of answering them. His eyes became lifeless and fixed as he randomly glanced around the room following nothing I could see and talking to nobody I could see. I was helpless and exasperated. I couldn't do anything to stop the auditory hallucinations.

I couldn't reach John and I didn't know how. I prayed incessantly, begging God each day to free me from anguish and to lessen the pain inside my heart. I was frightened. I feared the future. I ruminated on both these feelings to the point of hopelessness. My fear of his mental illness was incredibly real. I suffered in private and silence. Fear, together with shock and disbelief, burned so fervently in my heart because there was nothing to do but watch and wait. In the meantime, my child continued to deteriorate, and I continued to pray.

Sometimes I felt foolish in prayer. I prayed and expected a miracle to happen, that somehow God would intervene on my behalf. I prayed I would awaken from that nightmare. I experienced a shame that pierced me, but nothing happened. My shame fed my guilt, guilt fed my shame, and around and around I went, feeling like I spent my days on a mental merry-go-round.

I laughed at myself because I thought if I repeated my requests often enough, my reality would change. Maybe this terrible illness would somehow go away and leave my son alone!

Somehow my prayer rituals proved soothing. I prayed every hour; I had to. It was the way I was raised.

I regrettably started losing patience during a period of time. John began to pace back and forth, left and right, in and out of the house. I could tolerate most of his pacing and some other random actions such as throwing his arms up in the air or strange arm gestures.

When his mind accelerated, the actions that followed made little sense to us.

One evening, John was sitting in his chair as we were watching *Law & Order* on television. He had a lifeless look in his eyes, and his crossed leg was bouncing up and down. "Can you stop bouncing your leg?" I yelled. Another time, when he was overly fidgety, I yelled, "Sit down! For Pete sakes, take something!"

I was livid that my son's life was reduced to just watching television. I tried to reason with myself. *He is ill. Bipolar disorder is a brain disorder. I understand that he's not in control of his mind. I understand that his medications can cause side effects. He's compliant with his medications. I'm so angry. This illness is not my son. This illness won't defeat me or take me from my son. This illness will provide strength for both of us.*

I tried to believe these affirmations. But days seemed to all run together and seemed to turn into months, and it became more and more apparent that John's mind, as we knew it, was leaving.

Later we understood why his agitation worsened at times. The ever-changing meds were either not working or they took way too long to kick in. Why couldn't these doctors get it right?

While both David and I gave John his medications, and made sure he took every single pill, we didn't know what to do when he didn't respond in a way that assured us he was getting better. I began to lose faith in my own expertise as a nurse, mother, and caregiver. I lost *all* faith in the psychiatric profession, that was for sure.

Not only did mental illness seize John's mind, it was affecting my entire family as well. My son James was gravely concerned about his brother. I heard a lot of fear in his voice when he called to ask about John. I think he was terrified with the possibility that he carried the gene for bipolar disorder, and that it could pop up out of nowhere like it had with his brother. I always reassured him I was there for him and always would be. He was desperately concerned about John, yet James could only be an observer because he was living and working in another state. Still, he held it together due to his strong nature and calm mind. Nevertheless, he hoped for a miracle, like we all did.

I became someone I didn't recognize. I became frozen in time. Nothing happened as a result of my incessant prayers. Feeling abandoned by my own faith, I became so despondent I knew I had to seek help.

I forced myself to see a nurse practitioner with whom I was familiar at my primary care physician's office. She assured me that if the anti-depressants she was going prescribe to me didn't make a difference in several weeks, we would try another. She also added that HIPAA laws would keep anyone from knowing I was on meds. I was grateful for that, since I saw it as a weakness that I had to take medication. It took some time for me to face the fact that I was depressed, and very close to becoming nonfunctional. Later I was grateful I honored that push to get help, and for once had kept my pride at bay.

CHAPTER 22

TERRELL

May 2007

ALTHOUGH JOHN WAS consistently taking his medication while he was home, his symptoms worsened. Why did we end up going from doctor to doctor, from psychiatrists to therapists? Why couldn't they get his medications right? The medications would take days or weeks to take effect and there was no way we could be assured they would improve his symptoms. For financial reasons, I decided to book an appointment for John with a psychiatrist through the free public mental health department. This was the turning point for all of us.

Doctor Sidhare was in her mid-forties and had graduated from the University of Pennsylvania. She spoke privately with John for a few minutes while I waited outside the room. She came out of her office and asked me to come in. The look on her face screamed what I already knew. John was severely psychotic and would probably get worse. Despite adhering to his medication schedule, somehow, someway, the psychosis was now unstoppable.

She pulled me aside and informed me that she was going to admit him to Terrell State Hospital for extended treatment. The hospital was located an hour and a half from home. Though it was originally built as a correctional facility, the hospital resembled a small college campus.

Once I checked John in and said my goodbyes, I decided I needed some rest. I made plans to visit the following evening. Overwhelmed at the thought of my son in a facility that used to house inmates and juvenile offenders, I talked to my mother on the drive home. She suggested it was time to find John a "special home." There was never a time I had considered that. Her words broke my heart, and I sobbed all the way home.

○○○

I could only conceptualize that John was psychotic, mentally ill, and perhaps it wasn't my fault. By that time, I had read a lot on bipolar illness and listened to doctors. This illness had a high genetic factor. Intellectually, I saw the illness and its evolution in my ex-husband and his mother. I saw how it came down the line. I had loved and lived with three people from three different generations for most of my life. Living day in and day out with mental illness did not at all match what it says in books, articles, online, and other resources. It occurred to me that much of what was reported wasn't evidence based. These were, for the most part, personal stories from individuals with a mental illness and served to comfort more than inform. What I had learned about mental illness was what I had read, seen in movies, what my mother had told me, and what I learned in a brief course in nursing school. No wonder I was a wreck!

I was more confused than ever for a couple of weeks after I left John at Terrell. I bombarded myself with so many thoughts and feelings that I couldn't label any single emotion to attempt to trace it back to its source. I despised the endless stream of uncontrollable thoughts. They wouldn't stop, no matter how hard I tried. I was so obsessed with fixing the situation, but

I couldn't even form a simple plan. I lost the ability to choose. Surely I had lost my mind and would soon live across the hall from John at Terrell. I thought it would be a much better life than I had at that point. I was leading a life so full of pain and disappointment I had to increase my dosage of antidepressants.

I kept all my feelings inside, fearing that if I tried to reach out to others they would blame me for John's illness. My family members were practically the only people who knew about John. I figured all others believed the stigma surrounding mental illness, that people with mental health issues were dangerous; they should be rejected; they are treated differently; they can't function in society; they made a conscious choice to be that way; they were treated badly by a parent as a child; they are possessed. The list goes on and on.

I realized that I too once felt that intensely about mental illness. Despite being a nurse, spending most of my days helping others recover from a physical illness, I discriminated against mental illness. I wasn't sure where these feelings were born. How had I stooped this low? How did these values, or lack thereof, happen? I really wanted to know why I felt this way. I somehow knew that these feelings kept me from helping my son, and myself, recover from our private hell. It was causing me to kick John out of my heart. That new knowledge about myself was like putting another log on a bonfire. The daily thoughts and worries doubled in frequency.

One day these feelings built such a powerful force inside of me I thought that I would explode. At the point of no return of that intense force, surprisingly, a powerful sense of peace fell over me, as if I were being held within loving arms. A beautiful memory surfaced and I closed my eyes to relish it.

I remember you, John, radiant and strong. The sun's rays are falling on our skin at Wildwood Beach. We are walking hand in hand on the beach while on vacation in late summer with your grandparents in New Jersey. I feel the cold, wet sand under my feet. I see your little tanned feet kicking at the waves. The droplets fall in slow motion. A warm, wet breeze blows against our skin. Despite the wind blowing sand in our eyes, we continue to walk beside the waves. I lose myself in the joy of being your mother. I lose myself at the thrill of you as my son. I am so blessed.

I understood then that beating myself up with guilt and shame wasn't working. These emotions only hindered John's progress and kept me from moving forward with my usual confidence in a crisis. I accepted these facts. When I believed this was the truth, the pain of carrying the emotional burden of John's illness began to fade. All my biases dropped away, and some positive force stepped in to guide me. It wasn't hope. It was a fresh new way of looking at John's illness in a new light. I began to feel like a huge miracle was on the horizon.

Father God, how do You want me to proceed now that I feel You near?

CHAPTER 23

NAMI

JOHN REMAINED IN treatment for five weeks. His progress was slow, but I started noticing a new sparkle in his eye. Sometimes I met with psychiatrists and counselors to discuss his medications and his current treatment plan.

Finally the social worker called me and informed me that John was ready to be discharged. He slept twelve hours a night and ate continuously for about a month. Untreated bipolar depression, over time, takes its toll. It ravaged my son in so many ways.

As John began to stabilize, his body began to heal. He gained ten pounds and continued to put on weight, his sleep improved, and his pacing ceased. David and I agreed to split responsibility for his care. I managed the doctor appointments, medications, side effects, symptoms, and took care of other personal care expenses. His father made sure he ate, took his medications, and monitored his symptoms such as behavior and sleep so if needed, we could intervene early and alert the doctor.

John required constant supervision and work, and our health suffered during this time. I was in my third semester of school and working on the topic for my dissertation. I was so exhausted all the time I was ready to drop out. John not only assured me he was going to work on getting well, he encouraged me not to drop out. As a result, he gave me hope.

He kept his word and did concentrate on getting well. We began to see the light of recovery.

While John was in Terrell for five weeks, my introduction to National Alliance on Mental Illness (NAMI) Family to Family classes came out of the blue. NAMI is a grassroots advocacy group for those with mental illness. One of my professor's colleagues, a mental health nurse practitioner, suggested a venue for me to talk about my son, his mental illness, and his past noncompliance to treatment. She was a good nurse and teacher and provided a sense of comfort for me. I had never heard of NAMI before John went to Terrell, and I was desperate to talk to a professional, to anyone at that point, who would who would listen about my son, his illness, and how his illness affected *my* life. Keeping all my feelings inside was just about to drive me crazy, and I knew it. I was open to my professor's suggestion.

OOO

Before NAMI, I began to understand my own biases and myths I held about mental illness. I thought I had freed myself from these feelings. But during the groups I saw how these myths imprisoned me and contributed to my self-loathing, guilt, and shame. I'd learned to accept certain stigmas from small-town values learned as a child, and I carried them with me until NAMI. That was the ball and chain I had carried while caring for three generations of family members whom I love. These feelings kept me from my own heart and created a chasm between John and me. Finally, I could move into understanding and compassion which was just below the surface of my wrong thinking.

Another miracle developed while our son was in the crisis of his life. My ex-husband and I didn't have much of a productive relationship during that last decade. When I first learned about family support from NAMI, I spoke to David about it. He listened but I figured he never thought any further past that conversation about NAMI and Family to Family classes for those of us affected by mental illness. I was overwhelmed when I saw him walk into the room where the first meeting was held. He sat across from me with other couples, and even introduced himself as a father who had a mother with a mental illness and he now had a son with mental illness.

A lot of pain surfaced during those eleven classes. David began understanding, more than anyone, how his blatant disregard to get help, and his inability to even acknowledge his own illness hurt me and his children. That was what broke our family apart.

Then he saw just how much his mother's mental illness affected him. His mother refused to take medication, and he suffered as a child because of it. I certainly blamed him for not being responsible enough to break that cycle. I blamed him for John's noncompliance. If his own mother refused treatment for her condition, her son would too. Noncompliance down the line practically ruined our lives. My ex and I finally learned a lot about mental illness and the stigmas that surround it.

The Family to Family classes were just what we both needed to move forward in support of ourselves and John. David and I healed the pain from our divorce. Once he shared the pain of his childhood with the other members, our agony lifted. His disclosure, and my relief and release of so much pain, began to transform our lives from fear and denial into loving people who could see past our own pain and focus on our son as a team. We learned ways to take care of ourselves during stressful times to come, and I learned to turn to David in times of stress during our caretaking times.

Near the end of the course, the group facilitators and a few other members said to me in front of the class, "You, Linda, are the next generation of NAMI. We see you as an advocate, and the next instructor of this class!"

What came next was a surprise to me and everyone in my life.

CHAPTER 24

LIFE AFTER MENTAL ILLNESS

Iᴛ ꜰɪɴᴀʟʟʏ ᴅᴀᴡɴᴇᴅ on me that when I found my son, I'd also found my life's purpose. Every crisis and the turmoil leading up to my son's diagnosis, homelessness, and recovery changed me in many ways. In 2010, I graduated with my PhD in Nursing *Research and Education*. As a direct result of my experiences as a mother of a son with bipolar disorder, my life is purposeful, working with students and parents and serving as an advocate for parents of children with mental illness. After the NAMI Family to Family classes, I became qualified to teach this class to other families. Next I became a state trainer, and in 2015, wrote my first book, *Breakthrough: Moving Beyond Your Mental Illness Diagnosis to Your Highest Functioning Outcome.*[3]

Currently I volunteer to serve on the state board of directors of NAMI, as a nurse, and to give voice to mothers of children with mental illness and advocate for mental health changes. In my professional life, I have been an assistant professor of nursing at Texas Women's University in Dallas, Texas, and fully engaged in teaching mental health nursing in the undergraduate nursing program and will continue in 2019.

I teach undergraduate nursing students how to care for psychiatric inpatients at a local facility, support jail diversion, mental health court, and am an advocate for local mental healthcare and medications for all in our county and state with mental illness. My advocacy is best served by opening the minds and hearts of nursing students and the nurses, many of whom are often unaware of their own biases about mental illness.

In May 2018, I transitioned from my teaching role to UT Southwestern in Dallas, Texas, as the Director of Nursing Research, building an infrastructure for nurses to conduct evidence-based practice projects and research studies. This role allows me more time to devote to mental health advocacy while I remain on the cutting edge of innovation in health-care research.

OOO

Long before John's mental illness I had some inkling that I was in service to others, but until that event, I was devoid of purpose, lost while I was looking for and awaiting my life's purpose to unfold.

Not once did it occur to me that my life's purpose would come from my experiences with John combined with all the other experiences of my life. I look back now and realize, I was traveling to my life's purpose all the time! I no longer look for security and safety from the outside to confirm my existence. Confronting myself, and my biases about mental illness, was *huge* for me, and as a result, my whole family healed.

Before John's mental illness, I struggled inside myself to hurry through life to get to the place I was desperately trying to find in order to learn my purpose. I had no idea why I had this feeling. One day as I was in church praying, I had an over-whelming feeling that my life was designed for one purpose, which was to serve others. That was the day I knew deep down inside that I was to follow in the footsteps of a long line of nurses, including my mother, and become a nurse. My life soon took on a different focus, a detour, a road that introduced me to people I know and love who are mentally ill. What started at age sixteen when I met my future mother-in-law began a series of events, I now know as my life's purpose, to the discovery that there is life after mental illness.

When I was introduced to mental illness in my teens, I was horrified and embarrassed to be in the presence of someone who was "not normal." I avoided any contact with someone who I thought was "slow." Watchful waiting and anticipating what might happen was the order of the day. While having a bite to eat with my future mother-in-law, a sound like a clanging plate or people shouting in a restaurant could turn delight to disaster in a moment. Now I can look at people with mental illnesses in the eye with respect to honor the dignity of their struggle.

As a registered nurse, I treated patients and counseled their families. Although I didn't specialize in psychiatric nursing, I began to see patients diagnosed with cancer were severely depressed. This depression would also show up in many members of their family. At that time, we didn't mention the word cancer. Sometimes even a wife or husband would take us aside and ask that we do not mention the "C" word to the patient. Patients and their loved ones were left to their own devices to deal with depression.

At one time a cancer diagnosis brought fear, and sometimes people with cancer were ostracized because some thought you could "catch" the disease. There was a stigma during the early 1980s with the AIDS epidemic, too. But with advocacy, grass-roots efforts, and organizations of passionate people, those stigmas have slowly dissipated. Despite all the patients I cared for, I may not have been empathetic enough because I did not know what it felt like to live in a world of stigma and shame from an unexpected or uninvited illness that could change your entire life.

Mental illness, from my experience, lingers in a shadow of intolerance, and society ostracizes those affected to this very day. I contributed to that thinking, because my family and individuals who I trusted and loved didn't know any different. Their biases about mental illness were passed down to me, society perpetuated these myths, and conflict about what was real grew inside of me.

My new experiences and becoming educated about mental illness changed me profoundly. Mental illness lingers in a shadow of untruths. My love for three generations of people who are mentally ill melted away my biases, and I learned the truth about mental illness for myself. It's a fact of life and a health issue, and it needs to be treated as such.

Before I understood mental illness, I thought I knew what love felt like. I know now that love is a feeling of pure bliss, continually flowing through and out of me, in search of people to share my love. My heart is wide open, available to all people who live in the world of mental illness. Not one day goes by that I am not in a conversation, giving a hug, sensing a heavy heart, encouraging anyone who shares with me they now live in a world of mental illness.

I am more compassionate, loving, happy, and joyful. Best of all, I know people with mental illness are lovable, kind, funny, and unique, and require all the love and compassion, tolerance, and inclusiveness you can give them!

CHAPTER 25

UNPREDICTABLE

THE DIAGNOSIS OF a mental illness in an adult brings many unknowns. Much research is available about the symptoms of bipolar illness, yet there are no definitive answers about what behaviors are clearly indicative of this illness.

The classic symptoms of bipolar disorder usually manifest in teenagers and young adults ages fifteen to twenty-four. They can have extreme sadness and a sense of hopelessness, lack of interest in activities that once intrigued them, lack of focus and concentration, high anxiety, and lack of sleep in the midst of extreme exhaustion. Then they can quickly cycle to mania, such as elevated moods with unrealistic, uncharacteristic, grandiose ideas accompanied by feverish activity to carry out these ideas even if there's no plan or resources to accomplish an unrealistic idea. I know of a fifty-six-year-old man whose bipolar symptoms manifested soon after his divorce. He had a court order to pay a huge amount of alimony and child support each month. He had a great job with a decent salary. Nevertheless, a grandiose idea came to him out of nowhere. He had a hobby of collecting antiques and strange collectables. He had a reasonable collection of them displayed in his home before his mission began. The idea was that he would open an antique store in the rural town where he lived (population seven thousand), with no large cities or towns nearby. This little town did not attract seasonal tourists. Deciding he needed more inventory he spent his weekends traveling to antique stores, many of which were hundreds of miles from his home.

This collection process went on for months. He failed to secure a storefront, stating that would be his last step. Gradually he spent most of his money, in addition to his retirement fund, on inventory. Months later, his enthusiasm gradually dissipated and reality and guilt set in. His friends urged him to see a doctor, who, thank God, was wise enough to see the symptoms of bipolar disorder. He was prescribed medication and stabilized somewhat. Now he has three huge storage lockers of bizarre items that he won't even look at because of the guilt and shame he feels from slipping into what he calls "insanity."

Looking back, I can see where and when my son's mania began. It was the time he borrowed three thousand dollars from his father to play the stock market with the goal of purchasing a new car. He was so pumped and ecstatic and more than confident that his plan would work.

Another incident was when he impulsively left for Milan just a few months before he was to graduate from law school. Both incidents concerned me a great deal because John had always been a meticulous planner. Red flags went up, but I was still in denial and justified his actions as blowing off steam from the stress he was experiencing from working so hard in school. Now I understand why these behaviors appeared. He was in the phase of bipolar manic madness.

It's anyone guess why or when bipolar illness will strike. Studies show that hormonal imbalances can trigger symptoms, as well as environmental factors, traumatic events, childhood abuse, a significant loss, and the list goes on. But the true question is, what is behind these reactions?

One indicator that I know for sure from studying psychiatric articles, workshops, continued education, and conversations with professionals, is that there is a genetic component.

There are *"five psychiatric disorders, attention deficit hyperactivity disorder (ADHD), autism (AUT), bipolar disorder (BD), major depressive disorder (MDD), and schizophrenia (SZ), which are highly heritable and polygenic."*[4] (Polygenic is defined as many genes in play for the condition to express itself.)

Strong predispositions to bipolar disorders in families has been proven through twin studies (Barnett and Smoller, 2009).[5] There have been many studies as to whether bipolar disorder is inherited from either parent. Some studies show it's more likely to be inherited from the mother, other research shows there's a higher risk of inheritance from the father. So your guess is as good as mine.

Bipolar disorder often runs in families, and the evidence suggests a genetic predisposition to the illness. A stressful environment, negative life events, or a "trigger," may interact with an underlying genetic or biological vulnerability and could result in a diagnosis of a brain disorder. There are other possible triggers of bipolar episodes. The treatment of depression with an anti-depressant medication may trigger a switch into mania, sleep deprivation may trigger mania, or hypothyroidism may produce depression or mood instability.

One in five adults, or 44.7 million Americans, experience a mental health episode in any given year.[6] Despite effective treatments, long delays are common between the first onset of symptoms and the time when people seek and receive treatment. Less than one-third of adults with a diagnosable mental illness receive mental health services. In the United States, the combined annual cost of mental illness is estimated to be seventy-nine billion dollars. Almost sixty-three billion dollars reflects the disability and loss of productivity because of these illnesses. Many of those diagnosed with mental illness are struck down in the prime of their life, and as a result, become a financial and emotional burden on their families through no fault of their own.

According to an article by attorney Joseph J. Wielebinski, and results from a Hazelden Betty Ford Foundation survey of eleven thousand five hundred attorneys in Washington State:

- Approximately 61 percent experienced concerns with anxiety

- Almost 46 percent acknowledged depression at some point in their career

- 16 percent reported experiencing social anxiety

- 12.5 percent experienced attention deficit hyperactivity disorder

- 8 percent experienced panic disorder and 2.4 percent experienced bipolar disorder

- More than 11 percent reported suicidal thoughts during their career[7]

There is a paucity of other research conducted on samples of attorneys about their mental illnesses. Unfortunately, the stigma still exists today in law, medicine, nursing, and other licensed professions, but less so than it did a decade ago. Despite the increased awareness of mental illnesses by the public and the efforts of many organizations, the myths about these conditions remain blatant in the workplace.

OOO

The triggers in John's diagnosis of bipolar disorder were a combination of factors including family history, genes, the stress of scholastic and financial burdens, and substance abuse, all of which worked to seize his rational mind and replace it with unpredictability. As disappointment surfaced, an ugliness started to fester inside of me, my joy of having a not-so-perfect son anymore crushed me. My transformation took place when anger, disappointment, and grief became the impetus to transform my life. I hope that sharing my story about my journey will lift you toward your child's possibilities.

Lost and Found was written over several years because of my own biases, stigma, and conflicts about coming out as a mother of a son living with a mental illness. I still hesitate to share my ex-husband's family history of mental illness. Although I am sharing my story, I am well aware of the stigma and bias that exist today and am prepared to tackle these alone. I know in the deepest part of myself, by exposing myself in this memoir, stigma about mental illness is lessened.

More importantly, my son supports this book, and is eager to share his story with you. Together as mother and son, we share our story to offer hope and inspiration to you and your loved ones so you too can move forward into action. This book is a commitment to this end. I decided to share my story and open myself both to resonate with mothers whose children are affected by mental illness and to demonstrate one person can change everything.

I acknowledge that I am a mother with a son diagnosed with a mental illness known as bipolar disorder, and now obsessive-compulsive disorder. I know what it feels like to be a mother who loves a child living with mental illness. What I know through research and study is that an individual is born with mental illness. I blamed myself for my son's illness for many years. My mantra today is: this illness was not my fault, nor did I cause it in any way, shape, or form. I suggest you affirm this to yourself daily. It will help you get yourself out of the way to take better care of your bipolar child and relieve unnecessary guilt.

CHAPTER 26

LOST OR PUNISHED?

ONE CAN ONLY imagine the number of families affected by this illness, and the problems they face trying to find help for their loved ones after reviewing the statistics in the previous chapter. What's even worse for some of those families is the fact that their loved ones with a bipolar disorder go missing. The United States defines a missing adult as one who is eighteen years or older and whose disappearance is voluntary or not. In 2014, the FBI reported 4,806 people with a mental or physical disability went missing. As of October 31, 2017, that number jumped to 31,417 missing. In the United States, there are about one hundred thousand missing person cases at any given time.

Table A-1: FBI National Crime Information Center (NCIC): Missing Entries of Adults Ages 18 and Older

Disability: a person of any age who is missing and under proven mental/physical disability or senile, thereby subjecting himself/herself or others to personal and immediate danger.	Total Missing Adults in Disability Category	Total Missing Adults	% Total Missing Adults
Cases (2012)	26,699	164,266	(16.3%)
Cases (2013)	26,342	165,344	(15.9%)
Cases (2014)	27,243	168,206	(16.2%)
Cases (2015)	28,059	174,209	(16.1%)
Cases (2016)	28,342	181,759	(15.6%)

8   Fernandes-Alcantara, A.L. U.S. Department of Justice, Federal Bureau of Investigation, 2012, 2013, 2014, 2015, and 2016 Missing Person and Unidentified Person Statistics Pursuant to P.L. 101-647, 104 Statute 4967, Crime Control Act of 1990 Requirements.

These statistics are troubling. Why is this definition stated as "missing with a suspected diagnosis of a mental disability?" It's clearly not definitive.

OOO

When my son went missing in 2007, it was a total surprise. He still wasn't well, but he was trying. He was compliant with taking his medication. He was seeing his psychiatrist on a regular basis, but two weeks after his hospitalization in New Jersey, he became extremely agitated and jumpy. When I saw his medication in the cabinet, I freaked. It didn't dawn on me at first to notify anyone. I knew the police would try to calm me down by informing me that he was an adult and could do as he pleased. I knew that route was hopeless. Adults with mental illness receive little coordinated effort through local, state, and federal agencies unless a crime is involved. Plus, I was still wrapped up in shame and stigma. I didn't want anyone, even the police, to know that he was a missing mentally ill person and couldn't care for himself properly.

I was fortunate that I only spent a few weeks of the two months when John went missing enduring intense agony of imagined, but very possible conditions and/or dreadful events that could have happened to him. I was informed by the police, hospitals, and urgent care units from time to time when he was sick or got in trouble in various cities he was wandering through. I had secretly placed my business card in his wallet. On the back of the card I wrote, "In case of emergency, call this number."

John was informed of the Health Insurance Portability and Accountability Act (HIPAA) by the hospital staff when he ended up in emergency rooms whether voluntarily or not when he went missing. He always signed a consent for me to be contacted. I was very grateful for these calls. When the phone rang, I was terrified and relieved at the same time. Navigating the mental healthcare system was daunting for me when John became ill. That was years ago. I hope that through reading my experiences you won't have such a hard time seeking good treatment.

If you are caring for an adult child with a mental illness, it's important to understand HIPAA, which is quite frustrating. While this law was put in place to protect patients' health information, it poses a huge problem for caregivers for the mentally ill. If your child is under eighteen, a hospital and/or private physicians can set up a treatment plan that includes psychiatric referrals, medication checks, and other concerns which can be shared with you. There is a possibility for a clear line of communication. After a minor is considered an adult, then HIPAA kicks in. The patient now has the right to give or refuse consent to share their information with you.

It is well known that mentally ill people run into trouble with the law more than any other group of people. *Torrey, Zdanowicz, Kennard et al.* (2014)[9] reported 20 percent of inmates in federal prison and 15 percent of inmates in state prison suffer from serious mental disorders. Inmates with mental illnesses do more time than the standard because their symptoms get worse when they no longer have access to their medicine. They might be so ill that they can't communicate what they need to anyone. County jails and prisons have very few qualified professionals to treat these inmates. The general staff isn't educated or properly informed on how to recognize the symptoms of mental illness. Therefore, many inmates suffer tremendously day after day until they are released, only to end up incarcerated again.

"The risk of being killed while being approached or stopped by law enforcement in any given community is sixteen times higher for individuals with untreated serious mental illnesses than for other civilians. One in four fatal law enforcement encounters involve an individual with a mental illness. One half of all law enforcement homicides ends their life from an individual with a psychiatric disease. The arrest-related death program operated by the Bureau of Justice Statistics within the US Department of Justice is the only federal database that attempts to systematically collect and publish mental health information about law enforcement homicides. The program was suspended in 2015 because the data available to the agency

was not credible enough to report." (Fuller, Lamb, Biasotti & Snook, 2015, p 1).[10]

Another interesting study in 2014 reported that out of 429 crimes, 143 offenders were diagnosed with a mental illness, 4 percent were related to psychosis, 3 percent were related to depression, and 10 percent were related to bipolar disorder. (Peterson, Kennealey, Skeem, Brey & Zvonkovic, 2014).[11]

My son was incarcerated once for being drunk and disorderly. He wasn't hurting anyone or himself. He was in the beginning stages of his illness at the time. Thank God it wasn't worse than that, or I might have lost him forever. It is of the utmost importance to keep good track of your adult child and if possible, whether or not they are actually taking their medication while they are stabilizing. When bipolar disorder morphs into psychosis, anything is possible.

CHAPTER 27

THE MYSTERY OF MEDICATION

WHEN MY SON was hospitalized at Terrell, the doctors were sure he was psychotic due to a severe reaction to his medications. The side effects were unbearable for him, I'm sure, and he was exhibiting some of the strangest behaviors I had ever seen in him.

Lithium, a mood stabilizer, is the most widely used medication to treat bipolar because it has been the most researched through patient study reactions and intense study of the chemical. It's been the first line of treatment for forty years. But for some patients, lithium has horrible side effects, which include acne, thyroid suppression, enormous weight gain, and possible renal impairment. There is a danger of lithium toxicity, which brings on a new set of problems. And researchers really have no idea why it works as a mood stabilizer. Studies show that lithium works for only one-third of patients for whom it is prescribed.

I heard one of my colleagues talking about a new research that follows lithium as it travels through the brain using a certain type of cell taken from bipolar patients who did or did not respond to lithium. The researchers found that a certain protein was dormant in the bipolar patient or didn't exist at all. This protein is related to communication between nerve cells. By introducing a certain substance, the cell responded to lithium. This opens a whole new can of worms and provides hope for potentially new medications with fewer side effects soon. Now we must have faith and work with what current research gives us and take it seriously.

Lithium takes around two to three weeks to work to control severe mania. In the meantime, providers will almost always have to prescribe additional medications while the lithium is taking effect such as potent antipsychotics and benzodiazepines. These also have side effects, so the patient is taken back and forth to the doctor for medication adjustments repeatedly until some semblance of stabilization is apparent. This medication adjustment is ongoing throughout the patient's life. John continued, on his own, to drive to his regular visits to his psychiatrist for therapy and medication adjustments. He learned how to look for and recognize unstable symptoms and respond accordingly. It is possible for your adult bipolar child to get on with their lives once the manic and/or depressive episode is stabilized and the medications take effect, but you must be very diligent in dispensing their medication and watch for behavior changes.

Often the patients want to abruptly cease their meds due to the side effects or they feel they aren't getting better quickly enough, so they will take matters into their own hands. They might become highly psychotic or go missing. It's ideal for them to live with you while they stabilize. If they are reluctant to go along with this plan or say they can follow a treatment program on their own, it is safe to go with your gut. Don't believe them, no matter how sincere or persuasive they sound. Remember, they are sick and can't make rational decisions on their own when in the state of severe mania, depression, or even psychosis, especially when they initially come home from the hospital. It's possible, in most states, to petition the courts for legal guardianship, which can be done without an attorney.

What is needed to do this is a detailed physician's statement within ninety days after your child has been diagnosed outlining why the individual is mentally incapable of living on their own and dangerous to themselves. It is helpful to produce arrest records, hospital stays, and other relevant information. There are forms available on state websites to begin the process. Another resource that is helpful about adult guardianship is NAMI. In my first book, *Breakthrough: Moving Beyond Your Mental Illness Diagnosis to Your Highest Functioning Outcome,*[12]I go into more detail about this subject. Chapter six in my first book provides strategies in understandable steps to address the various issues that every caregiver encounters so they can navigate through the journey helping their loved ones. It also details crisis intervention plans that truly work.

CHAPTER 28

CARE FOR CAREGIVERS

CAREGIVERS ARE CONFRONTED with shock and disbelief with a diagnosis of a mental illness. The emotions and confusion can be overwhelming. I experienced how my own stigmas kept me from seeking relief from the chaos of horror, fear, and helplessness that overwhelmed me day after day. Therefore I was alone, which made the pain unbearable.

When my son was hospitalized the final time in Terrell, I had clear communication with his doctors and hospital staff. Needless to say, his time in Terrell gave me the break I needed to regroup and form a plan to help myself. This was when I connected with NAMI and opened myself up to their advice and counseling. By implementing their suggestions, I discovered that the symptoms I experienced meant I was experiencing caregiver burnout. Caregiver burnout occurs because we are ill-equipped to deal with the normal feelings of helplessness of just how we can face the fact that we are dealing, and will deal, with a loved one diagnosed with a mental illness. I advise that once this condition happens to you, reach out for help as soon as possible.

Caregiver "burden" is an understatement when it comes to mental illness. It's not like you can use technology and text, call, or email your loved one because often they are hospitalized and their state of mind is awry. Sometimes you'll have no idea where they are or what they are doing to support them.

Eighty-four million people in the United States are providing care for individuals with a mental health condition[13]. According to National Alliance for Caregiving, *On Pins and Needles: Caregiver of Adults with Mental Illness* (2016), [14] Americans who provide care to a child or an adult with a mental health condition, are physically and financially under stress and strain. Many reported emotional stress in addition to physical and financial strain as a result of their caregiving. Most reported an average of thirty-one hours a week of care compared to the average caregiver in the United States, who provides twenty-four hours of care per week. A total of 48 percent of caregivers reported that stigma prevented them from discussing their loved one's mental health issues with others, compounding their stress and strain and contributing to their feelings of isolation.

The results of a search of the literature revealed research about caregiver burden in mental illness is lacking. In fact, when I conducted a quick review of the literature for research studies about caregiver burden over a five-year span (2012–2017) using the keywords "mental illness," "research," and "caregiver burden," the search resulted in seven articles, none of which were related to mental illnesses, with only one research article on a collaborative care intervention. There were not any on interventions for caregiver burden in mental illnesses.

While this was a simple review of a couple of databases, what is interesting is almost all of the research about caregiver burden is on caregivers proving care for individuals with chronic conditions, not mental illnesses. The articles from the search confirm caregiver burden in mental illness exists, though few studies test interventions to decrease the burden. Of the seven articles, six include caregiver burden in Alzheimer's, dementia, oncology, and congestive heart failure populations (CINAHL). This is not an exhaustive literature search, but you get the idea.

One article's findings demonstrate anger and quality of life is lower in caregivers in the United States and other countries who care for loved ones with a mental illness (Bedemli, K., Lok, N., & Kilic, 2017).[15]

Breakthrough, my first book, is for caregivers, and chapter five is dedicated to caregiving. It includes strategies for caregivers to cope (Denke, 2015 p 41).[16]

○○○

When my son had his initial episode, I instantly became a caregiver of my son, who was graduating law school. I was horrified at the thought my son had a mental illness and frightened because I had no training in caring for someone with a mental illness.

Although my first exposure to someone with mental illness was in high school, and I experienced building a relationship with someone diagnosed with a mental illness, I was not their primary caregiver. I could leave and disengage from their illness at will. The fact that my son was diagnosed with a mental illness brought with it a responsibility and a burden that my life was no longer my own.

Secondly, not only would my life change, but I had little if any control over the way forward for me and my son. My initial thinking was one of pride and now I was horrified and frightened. I was horrified because of what people would think and how my son and I would be viewed, and frightened because of the isolation and stigma surrounding anyone diagnosed with a mental illness. So I understand what you are feeling at some level.

One professional couple, a physician and engineer with two sons, shared with me that when one son was diagnosed with a mental illness, they'd wished to know how to make the condition go away. They shared their initial horror and the disdain of learning their son was diagnosed with a mental illness and their shattered dreams of him being "professionally successful." Other families said that their unaffected sons or daughters want nothing to do with their brother or sister when they learn they have been diagnosed with a mental illness for fear they will be confronted with the reality they or their children may "catch" or also be diagnosed with the illness. Caregivers are confronted by shock and disbelief about the diagnosis, and because of stigmas, nonexistent in other diagnosed conditions, the horror, fear, and isolation that comes from feeling helpless and alone.

Strategies

Caregiver burden occurs most often because we feel helpless and out of control because of the unpredictability of caring for a loved one with illness, not just mental illness. If you concentrate on learning all you can and caring for yourself before your loved one, the burden will lesson because you have more control. My personal strategies to deal with caregiver burden include journaling, meditation, prayer, goal setting, sharing within my network, focusing on what I can control, attending NAMI support groups and Family to Family education classes, and mostly forgiving myself and practicing the strategies I list in my book to alleviate caregiver burden (Denke, 2015, p 43).[17] Using technology has been an excellent strategy to keep in contact with my son. This alleviates much anxiety for me. The most important lesson I learned is reminding myself I am not to blame for my son's illness. Guilt is a common feeling for parents and I believe this is because of stigma.

CHAPTER 29

FAITH

FROM 2002 THROUGH 2007, a loving bond with my son and daily prayer helped me cope with John's diagnosis. Although I have no concrete scientific proof, I believe that prayer changed the course of my son's illness and led to his successful turn-around. Other factors I attribute to his recovery are his high intellectual function, my nursing profession training, and a lot of resilience. Hopefully, this book will offer a way forward for other mothers in their search for their loved one's recovery. In *Breakthrough*,[18]there are many strategies included in toolkits at the end of each chapter for families to reference if their loved ones are diagnosed with mental illness.

Although prayer is not for everyone, Doctor Larry Dossey, an imminent physician, believes one's state of mind can greatly affect the body. He notes individuals can mentally send healing intentions to another even when separated or on different continents. The successful strategy involves some blurring of identities between receiver and sender and the health outcomes of the intended improve. And of course, this is also the recipe for any form of love, the surrender of self-centered interests of one partner in favor of the other.[19]

A study by HCD Research and the Louis Finkelstein Institute for Religious and Social Studies of the Jewish Theological Seminary conducted a survey of eleven hundred physicians in all specialties and found that 74 percent believe that so-called "miracles" have occurred in their past experiences, and that 73 percent believe they can occur today. Fifty-nine percent of these physicians said they pray for their individual patients, and 51 percent said they pray for their patients as a group.[20]Most physicians would likely agree with Saint Augustine that so-called "miracles" do not contradict nature, but they do contradict what we know about nature.

According to a 2015 Gallup poll, 75 percent of Americans identify themselves as Christians.[21]Spiritual events are documented to take place every day all over the world. Many of these experiences unfold because of a traumatic event, similar to being diagnosed with a mental illness.

When a loved one is diagnosed with a mental illness, traumatic events occur. This diagnosis creates a movement towards a transformation of one kind or another, and in some way, a shift will occur. The individuals who experience this event, and the loved one who is the diagnosed, are altered in some fundamental way and the dyad changes over time. I know this as a spiritual transformation.

A spiritual transformation involves a shedding of the old ways or experiencing an epiphany of some kind. An epiphany is a divine or heavenly understanding that is individual in nature but is best defined as a celestial experience leaving behind an altered form of self. Even for the non-religious, an epiphany is a new way of understanding themselves and the world that can't be denied. A person changes in a fundamental way of believing and behaving, which is different from an improved version of their former self. Many individuals, like me, also experience this change when someone they love is diagnosed with a mental illness and what follows. My son and I have a deep, fundamental connection. When he was diagnosed with bipolar disorder, we both began to change together. We morphed from our old, worn-out beliefs to new ways of believing and thinking about the world and ourselves.

In another research study, eighty-four patients were studied who were in treatment for depression at a natural-istic clinic. These patients met the diagnosis criteria for major depression and were prescribed selective serotonin reuptake inhibitors (SSRIs) over a period of eight weeks. Patients were evaluated at a baseline before treatment. After treatment, they were evaluated using the Montgomery Asberg Depression Rating Scale, the Beck Hopelessness Scale, the Dysfunctional Attitude Scale, and the Spiritual Orientation to Life scale. The researchers also asked whether the participants believed in God. (Perselow, Sarah, Lopez, Besada, & Islak, 2014).[22] The results indicated a significant reduction of depression symptoms and distortions. Every measure improved over the course of eight weeks for those patients who were more spiritual according to MADRAS scores. However, a belief in God did not correlate with a significant change in hopelessness or dysfunctional attitudes, although the mean change in scores was numerically greater for believers. This evidence suggests that caregivers who rely on their spirituality could have a spiritual transformation as the patient's illness evolved. The evidence could also demonstrate that for some individuals in recovery from mental illness spirituality is the primary element that contributed to their recovery.

For caregivers as well as loved ones, the diagnosis of mental illness can act as an impetus for a transformation of some kind to occur. This shift, or transformation, can alter the fundamental way the individual will experience and interpret future life events.

CHAPTER 30

I AM JOHN

I HAD INCIDENTS of mania and depression in high school. I would stay up all night and become depressed when things were not working out with a girl. I would either get really excited about something or really depressed about something. These swings would last unusually long periods, sometimes for a whole semester. I tried to hide these feelings from my mother because I knew it would worry her. I just didn't talk about it.

I kept unusual hours during college. I would sleep during the day and stay up all night watching television while I was living in the dorms. I also traded stocks my first year of college by day trading with large amounts of borrowed money. This continued for the semester until I lost approximately thirty-six thousand dollars on a short sale trade. Then that second year, I kind of got involved with a bad crowd. We would drink and use drugs. I would still get depressed, but I would self-medicate with substance use. That was kind of the reason behind it.

After college, I went to law school. The first year was pretty normal. I would still drink, but I didn't have too many symptoms except for depression. The second year, when the mania started, I started to feel a high level of self-esteem, like I was famous and everyone knew me. This compelled me to go out all the time and stay out all hours of the night even after everybody had gone home. It was kind of fun being excited about things, but it seemed as if it would never end. I would end up going through all my money, and ignored all my responsibilities, like school. I became aggressive towards people. I would either offend them or tell them off. Often, I found myself being the exact opposite from the person I had known myself to be.

I had a girlfriend at the end of the second year, which calmed me down. But when we broke up six months later, I became depressed and stayed that way for a year. That was abnormal, I think. Also, I failed one of my classes and had to go to school that summer. I think that added to the depression. It was probably because I was manic the time before, and I wasn't paying attention to my studies like I should have been. After I caught up with all my classes in that last semester, another manic episode began.

At first it wasn't so bad, I was just excited about things again. Then I traveled overseas with a new girlfriend and I thought I was famous again. That time was more intense, and it snowballed when I got back to school. Eventually, after staying up several days in a row, my roommate had to admit me to the hospital for putting a knotted hose around his dog's neck. I was there for two weeks, and they prescribed lithium.

After I graduated, I moved back to Shreveport, Louisiana. I was stable for about a year. I continued to drink, which resulted in a move to Dallas in the middle of the night. I stayed with friends, got a job, and stopped taking my medication. After about six months of feeling normal, I became manic again. I made an impulsive decision to move to New York! You can see a pattern here going from place to place. Once I moved there I got back on lithium but I continued to drink. This caused me to hear voices. I was hospitalized for a second time after throwing a computer out of a second story window in the apartment I sublet.

They put me on Geodon in New York, but it had some nasty side effects, so I stopped taking it. I did not move back to Texas, but soon left to wander the streets. I think it was hard to stay in one place because I was not stable, and it was difficult to stay indoors. I couldn't even just sit for long, I had to be all over the place. I would hitch rides with various people with bad intentions, like looking for sex or to rob me. Not all the people who helped me were bad. Some were genuinely concerned for my well-being. I made my way to Florida by hitchhiking. There, I lived in a mall parking lot, stealing meals from the food court during the day, and stealing alcohol and cigarettes from local stores in the area. I was again hospitalized after trying to steal some clothes from a Target store by getting naked and putting them on in the middle of the store.

The hospital staff eventually sent me back to Texas with prescriptions for Depakote and Risperdal. That combination started working well for me, and I could work again. I have been stable since then, and that was 2007. The only thing that has emerged since then was a diagnosis of obsessive compulsive disorder, which I was told in the hospital was a possibility. I was prescribed an antidepressant for that. Besides that, some aspect might act up every year or so, but if I stay in contact with my psychiatrist and take care of it right away, it might not cause a major interruption in my life.

In conclusion, I advise anyone who has a mental illness to take their medication regularly, and *not* drink or do drugs.

OOO

From 2007 until now, I am doing quite well in many aspects of my recovery. I practice law and work in my own practice, and for almost four years, from 2012 to 2015, I worked in a small family law firm. In 2011, I was having periodic anxiety, and these anxiety attacks worsened over the next year while I was in court, which was occurring at least three or four days a week.

Once the anxiety attacks worsened, I developed both anxiety and panic attacks, untreatable with medication. My decision for myself required me to quit my job and become homebound for a few months, and intensive modifications to medications.

My psychiatrist figured out that I had an obsessive-compulsive disorder and prescribed an antidepressant to treat it. This helped me get out of the house and back to work. I joined a firm in 2012 and worked there for the next four years, until the end of 2015, without incident until I had a three-day jury trial and did not sleep at all for a thirty-six-hour period. This caused me to begin having mania. I eventually had to take a leave of absence from my job after reducing my antidepressant to control the mania.

In 2018, I decided to make a career decision mostly because of my condition, but there is another reason. As an attorney in my own practice, I was burned out. There are several reasons for this burnout: the courtroom appearances were becoming more and more overwhelming for me and medication my physician prescribed caused a rebound of my bipolar mania, which is not a symptom I can manage without a medication change. This was not as easy as it sounds because an antidepressant can cause my mania to manifest and that is what happened. When my physician stopped this medication, my anxiety became a problem in court. Secondly, I am empathetic by nature and I can take on the client's problems from either their divorce or custody.

I understand this is not the client's doing, or something that the client brings on themselves but oftentimes it is brought about by a spouse or ex-spouse or a family member and comes out of the blue. I decided I would make a change in my career trajectory and pursue other types of law which do not require court room appearances.

On the advice of my family and some of my mentors, I decided to apply for law positions in compliance and landed a wonderful opportunity at a large insurance company. I have never been happier. This type of law requires me to use my law degree but does not require courtroom appearances. My work is interesting and has many benefits such as working with other attorneys similar in nature to myself, and all the perks of working for a large company including upward mobility. I am grateful for my work, because it is a great source of satisfaction for me and a large part of my life.

My condition continues to require me to be vigilant and watch my diet, get enough sleep, and monitor any new stressors which occur in my life which alter my brain chemistry for one reason or another. My mother and father, together with my psychiatrist, all play an essential role watching for any behavior changes or listening for changes in speech, such as its cadence or topics which seem out of the ordinary for me, ultimately stepping in and asking me to intervene. When my parents ask me to intervene, this requires me to call my psychiatrist, and he usually makes an adjustment in my medications.

My bipolar condition requires my constant attention just when I think I got this thing under control I notice changes in my symptoms and must make a small adjustment. One example of a change is the fact that I am aging and my body is changing. Another example is I recently lost forty pounds because of reductions in my medications. But I feel better and know in the beginning when I was compliant on my medications, the extra weight was not easy for me to accept because I have always been in shape and quite agile most of my early life. This was so difficult. But it was a tradeoff and now after almost a decade, I am stable enough and because of my relationship with my physician he supports me by attempting to taper off some of my medications.

Like any chronic condition, I notice just when I begin to experience some calm and regularity in my life, inevitably an old symptom arises which was in check, seems to crop up all of a sudden out of the blue. With continued family support, medications, maintaining my routines, getting enough rest, limiting toxic people or situations, and having resources such as my insurance benefit, life is pretty good. More importantly, I am stable and working.

In late 2018, something noteworthy happened. Despite what you read in the textbooks about the odds of siblings diagnosed with bipolar disorder, my mother and father now have both of their boys, me and my brother, diagnosed with bipolar disorder. My brother is currently being treated for his bipolar disorder and doing good on his medication. This time, we all knew what to do, what to ask for, assumed our roles, and pulled the trigger early enough. His road trip was short-lived, unlike mine, and the financial losses were kept to a minimum. My brother started treatment early enough not to cause too much suffering for us. We all worried about him, but knowing what to do was essential to minimizing the suffering and damage these conditions can lead to if they remain untreated.

This is our hope for you. We hope you will find in this memoir ways to incorporate some or all of these strategies to help your loved ones as we did, but hopefully find a smoother path forward toward better mental health.

The following is a timeline of my major bipolar crisis episodes, where they occurred, and the expenses involved.

APPENDIX A

EMERGENCY AND INPATIENT EVENTS

2005–2015

Date of Encounter	Type of Encounter	State Where Encounter Occurs	Amounts	Outcomes
4/1/2005	Emergency Department	Louisiana	17,809.70	Indigent care
4/4/2005	Diagnostic Tests	Louisiana	720.01	Indigent care
12/15/2006	Emergency Department	New Jersey	1180.00	Indigent care
1/20/2007	Emergency/Outpatient	Texas	4589.00	Paid Cash
2/08/2007	Emergency Department	Alabama	885.51	Indigent Care
3/4/2007	Emergency Department and Inpatient	Florida	698.00 11,594.98	Indigent Care
3/9/2007	Physician	Florida	1200.00	Paid Cash
3/11/2007	Outpatient	Texas	150.00	Indigent Care
3/26/2007	Inpatient	Texas	24,000.00	Indigent Care
6/12/2007	Dentist	Texas	1232.00	Paid Cash
12/12/2007	Dentist	Texas	249.00	Paid Cash
2008–2015	Outpatient	Texas	5,025.00	Paid Cash

BIBLIOGRAPHY

Chapter 11
1   Rudowitz, R., Rowland, D. and A. Shartzer, "Health Care in New Orleans Before and After Hurricane Katrina," *Health Affairs*, August 29, 2006. Representatives March 13, 2007.

Chapter 20
2   "The Florida Mental Health Act "Baker Act," *Sections 394.451-394.47892, F.S.* https://www.dcf.state.fl.us/programs/samh/MentalHealth/laws/bainvex.pdf

Chapter 24
3   Denke, L. (2015). *Breakthrough: Moving from YOUR Mental Illness Diagnosis Toward YOUR High Functioning Outcome*, February 2, 2015. Total Publishing and Media http://www.totalpublishingandmedia.com/

Chapter 25
4   Wang, T., Zhang, X., Li, A., Zhu, M., Liu, S., Qin, W. Li, J., Yu, C., Jiang, T., & Liu, B. 2017; p 441. "Polygenic risk for five psychiatric disorders and cross-disorder and disorder-specific neural connectivity in two independent populations." *NeuroImage*. Clinical, ISSN: 2213-1582, Vol: 14, Page: 441-449.

5   Barnett, Jennifer H, and Jordan W, Smoller. "The Genetics of Bipolar Disorder." *Neuroscience* 164.1 (2009). 331–343. *PMC*. Web.

6   "Any Mental Illness Among Adults." Retrieved July 5, 2018, from https://www.nimh.nih.gov/health/statistics/mental-illness.shtml

7   Wielebinski, J. J., "Culture Shock: A groundbreaking empirical study confirms that lawyers face unprecedented substance abuse and mental health challenges." *Texas Bar Journal*,

2016. Accessed July 4, 2018 at https://www.texasbar.com/AM/
Template.cfm?Section=Table_of_contents&Template=/CM/
ContentDisplay.cfm&ContentID=32751 at www.http://
TexasBar.com

Chapter 26

8   Fernandes-Alcantara, A.L. *Missing Adults: Background, Federal
    Programs, and Issues for Congress.* Congressional Research
    Service by the U.S. Department of Justice, Federal Bureau of
    Investigation, Criminal Justice Information Services Division on
    December 26, 2007. Retrieved July 7, 2018 from https://fas.org/
    sgp/crs/misc/RL34616.pdf

9   Torrey EF, Zdanowicz MT, Kennard AD, et al. "The treatment of
    persons with mental illness in prisons and jails: A state survey."
    Arlington, VA, Treatment Advocacy Center, April 8, 2014.

10 Fuller, D.A., Lamb, H. R., Biosotti, M., & Snook, J. "Overlooked
    in the undercounted: The role of mental illness in fatal law
    enforcement encounters." *Treatment Advocacy Center.* Retrieved
    http://www.treatmentadvocacycenter.org/storage/documents/
    overlooked-in-the-undercounted.pdf

11 Peterson, J.K., Kennealey, P., Skeem, J., Brey,B., & Zvonkovic, A.
    "How often and how consistently do symptoms directly precede
    criminal behavior among offenders with mental illness?" *Law
    and Human Behavior.* (2014). Vol 38, No 5., 439–449. Retrieved
    at http://www.apa.org/pubs/journals/releases/lhb-0000075.pdf

Chapter 27

12 Ibid.

Chapter 28

13 "Caregiving in the U.S." Retrieved November 7, 2018 from
    https://www.caregiving.org/wp-content/uploads/2015/05/2015_
    CaregivingintheUS_Final-Report-June-4_WEB.pd

14 National Alliance on Caregiving: *On Pins and Needles:
    Caregivers of Adults with Mental Illness.* February 2016,
    Greenwald & Associates. Retrieved July 7, 2018 from https://

www.caregiving.org/wp-content/uploads/2016/02/NAC_Mental_
Illness_Study_2016_FINAL_WEB.pd

15 Bedemli, K., Lok, N., & Kilic. "Relationship between caregiver
burden and anger level in primary caregivers of individuals with
chronic mental illness." *Archives of psychiatric nursing*, 2017;
31(3), 263-68.

16 Ibid.

17 Ibid.

Chapter 29

18 Ibid.

19 Dossey, Larry, M.D. (2014). Interview by Doctor
Kausthub Desikachar, *The Power of Healing Intention.*
Retrieved from http://www.synergies-journal.com/
synergies/2014/9/21/0mt2rks8ezusj9oxvs1paexbz5bvcl

20 "Science or Miracle? Holiday season survey reveals physicians'
views of faith, prayer and miracles." *Business Wire*, 2004;
December; Retrieved at https://www.businesswire.com/news/
home/20041220005244/en/Science-Miracle-Holiday-Season-
Survey-Reveals-Physicians from http://www.jtsa.edu/

21 Gallup Poll December 2015. *Percentage of Christians in U.S.
drifting down, but still high.* Retrieved from https://news.gallup.
com/poll/187955/percentage-christians-drifting-down-high.aspx

22 Perselow, E., Sarah, P.I., Lopez, E., Besada, A., & Islak, W.W.,
"The impact of spirituality before and after treatment of major
depressive disorder." *Innovation in Clinical Neuroscience*, 2014;
Mar-Apr; 11(3–4): 17–23. Retrieved from https://europepmc.org/
backend/ptpmcrender.fcgi?accid=PMC4008297&blobtype=pdf

ACKNOWLEDGMENTS

WRITING THIS BOOK allowed me to examine my old, worn-out beliefs about mental illness and become an advocate for the mentally ill and their families.

It has been a difficult but highly rewarding personal transformation.

I am more than grateful for my son John. Without his willingness to allow me to assist him through his journey through his own mental illness, I might never have discovered my own life's purpose. His process guided me to my life's purpose and to return to my authentic spirit.

Gratitude goes to National Alliance on Mental Illness (NAMI) whose gentle persuasion guided me to healing myself and my family.

Finally, I thank the staff of Dupree Miller and Associates and the staff of Savio Publishing for their enthusiasm, support, and guidance to complete *Lost and Found: The Journey through My Son's Mental Illness.*

ABOUT THE AUTHOR

DOCTOR LINDA M. DENKE, PhD, RN, CCRC, is the director of nursing research at UT South-western Medical Center in Dallas, Texas. She is passionate about research and is actively engaged in designing nursing research studies, and curricula in research education, training, coaching, mentoring, innova-tion, and excellence. Her roles include principal investigator and co-investigator in nursing research, and to this end, using the findings in health promo-tion, prevention, and family engagement toward better family health outcomes.

Her earlier nursing roles focused on vulnerable popula-tions, including the Navajo people, and as a volunteer medical missioner in 2018 with Bless the Children in Menara, Kenya. She resides in a suburb outside Dallas, and is actively involved in mental illness advocacy as a member at large of the board of directors for National Alliance of Mental Illness of Texas. She is an avid equestrian in dressage and her desire is to provide care and training for horses with sports injuries to return to their former quality of life.

She is the author of *Breakthrough: Moving Beyond Your Mental Illness Diagnosis to Your Highest Functioning Outcome.*

Lost and Found: The Journey through My Son's Mental Illness is her second book.

Linda describes the burden of knowing there is a genetic predisposition for bipolar disorder, the shadow knowing casts on her life, and her struggle between joy and devastation that the birth of her child brings into her life. She discloses her aggrieved outlook on life as she awaits the moment her beloved son is diagnosed with bipolar disorder. Recently, to her surprise, her younger son was diagnosed with bipolar disorder, taking medication and doing quite good.